AF480727

# CONQUERING THE PATHWAY

*"To all those who still walk in search of their own horizon: this book is for you."*

JOSÉ GALVÁN

# PROLOGUE

# ON THE THRESHOLD OF THE PATH

There are paths traveled with the feet, and others that are only traveled with the soul. Conquering The Pathway is born from this second type: from those invisible trails where what is learned weighs more than what is walked, where each step holds a whisper, a wound, a revelation. This book does not intend to teach, but to accompany; it does not seek to guide, but to remind us of what we sometimes forget: that life is a journey made of light and shadow, of beginnings and farewells, of innocence that is born and wisdom that fades to be reborn in others.

Imagine, for a moment, being able to contemplate your own life from two perspectives, two different angles, or two seemingly opposite stages: the childhood that dreams and the old age that understands. That is what Conquering The Pathway offers through a child who begins and an old man who ends: different experiences, opposing expectations, yet united by the same footsteps and the same traces left behind for those who can find in them a reflection, a coincidence, or an echo of themselves. They walk together, not because destiny demands it, but because life knows that every human being is built between what they were and what they aspire to become.

Here, each chapter is a small window open to the soul. The stories reveal that wisdom doesn't belong only to those who have lived long lives, nor hope only to those just beginning: both dwell within us all, striving to meet at the heart's core. Sometimes the child teaches what the elder has forgotten; sometimes the elder remembers what the child doesn't yet know. But always, with each step, both discover that life is a mirror that shatters only to show us more facets of the same truth.

This book speaks of the love that saves, the pain that transforms, the faith that sustains, the time that wears us down, and, at the same time, heals us. It speaks of that mysterious learning that accumulates silently as we walk, without even realizing it. And, above all, it speaks of the inner journey each person undertakes when they dare to look back without resentment and forward without fear.

Those who read these pages may find solace, may find questions, may find companionship for their own path. But if there is one thing I deeply desire, it is that, upon finishing, you understand that there is no small path or useless step. Each stretch, however insignificant it may seem, is part of the great conquest: that of knowing oneself, accepting oneself, and continuing to move forward.

Because in the end, the path is not conquered with the feet… It is conquered with the soul.

# TABLE OF CONTENTS

# INTRODUCTION

Conquering the Pathway is a book of reflection and inner growth that invites readers to see life as a path traveled step by step, with effort, setbacks, lessons, and hope. Through symbolic and profound stories, the work intertwines two opposing yet complementary perspectives: that of a child and that of an elderly person. These are two distinct stages of life, with different expectations and experiences, yet both are marked by the same footprints on the path.

Each chapter addresses universal themes such as truth, wisdom, work, freedom, silence, loss, perseverance, pain, tolerance, compassion, dreams and memories, resilience, and death. The characters and situations represent real human struggles: sowing without knowing whether there will be a harvest, rising after a fall, and continuing onward even when the weariness of the soul weighs more heavily than that of the body.

The book conveys a clear message: no matter where one begins or how long the journey may seem, the essential thing is not to abandon the path. The footprints left by those who came before become a guide for others, reminding us that living with purpose, humility, and hope is, in itself, the greatest conquest.

# CHAPTER I

# THE ENCOUNTER AT THE BEGINNING OF THE JOURNEY

It was a long road through time. Its passage seemed endless, so long it vanished into the horizon, its end seemingly unreachable. It lay there, stretching like a gray ribbon that disappeared where the sky and earth appeared to meet. No one knew where it truly began or where it ended. Only that it was alive, changing with every step.

The path was dusty and under a merciless sun. That same sun, which barely bid farewell to the morning with an indifferent greeting. Despite the heat, the earth still held the coolness of dawn, and a gentle breeze stirred the leaves as if the road itself wished to say hello.

The boy arrived first. He carried a wooden toy in his pocket, a curious gaze, and the innocence of one who still believes that anything is possible.

He stopped in front of the entrance: a stone archway weathered by time and covered in dry leaves. He hesitated for a moment, unsure whether to cross.

Then, he spotted the old man in the distance. He seemed part of the landscape: still, serene, and as worn by time as the rocks that surrounded him. His steps were slow and deliberate, yet firm, as if each one told a story of victories and defeats.

The boy hesitated, wondering whether to wait for him or not, but curiosity won out over fear.

When he stood before him, he discovered that the old man's eyes were ageless. They were like ancient mirrors where time had learned to remain silent. The wrinkles of time were etched on his face, but so too did a serenity shine, a serenity that only years can bestow. In his hand, he carried a walking stick worn smooth by years, and by other paths he had already traveled.

The boy looked at him with distrust, and the old man smiled calmly.

Are you lost? The old man asked.

The boy shook his head.

I'm not lost... I just don't know where I'm

going.

The old man smiled.

Then you're exactly where you're supposed to be.

Where are you going? The boy asked timidly.

Wandering along the path, lad, the old man replied with a slight smile.  The path itself shows me where to go.

Are you going to cross the archway?  the boy asked.

I hope so, the old man replied.  But a path is never conquered alone.

And what is the name of this path? The boy asked.

As the old man calmly replied, at his own pace:  Generally, travelers have to figure it out for themselves.

But how can you know the name of a path? the boy asked again.

As you walk, no one will have to answer. If

you pay attention, the answer will come on its own, the old man replied energetically.

As you walk, you will discover that the ground beneath your feet seems to transform, he added. What seemed rough becomes firm, and what seemed far away begins to be within reach. The first step, however small, contains the seed of all victories. That is to say, no one conquers a horizon all at once, but little by little.

Upon hearing the old man's answer, his curiosity continued to grow, and he asked again:

And at what point along the path can I find out its name? The old man smiled and said: That's exactly what I was asking at your age. We walk searching for answers, even though every step is a mystery.

Could you explain again why we walk, Grandfather? the boy asked, his voice trembling. The old man smiled, unbothered. Because walking is how life teaches us. Every step is an open book, and every stone on the path is a word written for us.

The boy lowered his gaze and looked at the ground. There he found almost faded animal tracks, dry branches and leaves, and tiny seeds from wild trees. Everything seemed to be telling him something he hadn't heard before.

So, the path speaks?  he persisted.

Yes, son, the old man replied.  It speaks with the voice of the wind, with the birdsong, with the stillness of the air, and with the desire to live. Only those who walk slowly and attentively can hear it. Only then will you discover that every footstep has an echo, that every breath infuses life, and that the horizon, though distant, will await you without haste.

The boy, intrigued by the old man's serenity, couldn't contain his doubts:

Aren't you afraid of getting lost?

Fear exists, of course, the old man answered. But the important thing isn't whether or not you get lost, but to keep moving forward and never give up. Every step leads us to a lesson, even if we don't yet know what it is.

The boy, still uncertain, observed the path that stretched out before him: uneven, mysterious, sometimes shrouded in shadows, and other times by rays of light that filtered through the clouds.

From the spark of interest in his eyes, one could deduce that he understood that the journey never begins abruptly, but with a silent decision that takes shape deep within the heart. And that walking is not merely moving, but rather to learn at every step.

Noticing the concern disguised as interest, the old man offered a deeper explanation:

Each initial step is like a declaration of faith, or an oath sealed in blood. You don't know exactly where it will lead you, but you must trust that moving forward is better than remaining still. At first, your thoughts are filled with doubt: Will I be able to do it? Is this effort worthwhile? However, you will soon understand that these questions are not answered before you walk, but rather along the way.

What if we stop? the boy asked, a hint of fear in his voice.

The old man looked at him gravely.

He who does not move forward falls back, and stagnant water rots. So too does the soul, if it ceases to move, wither.

The boy looked down at his barely worn

shoes and then gazed at the horizon. He placed his hand on his chest and held within him those words he did not yet understand, but which one day would blossom in his heart.

The old man extended a trembling hand, and the boy, after a moment, took it.

I won't let go, he said.

At that moment, the old man raised his eyes to the sky. He remembered other beginnings, other paths, other companions who had already faded into the distance. His eyes, however, showed not sadness, but gratitude.

And with a gentle squeeze, he replied:

There's no need to let go… the path itself will one day teach us each to follow our own way. In this journey, we all play a part.

From that moment, they agreed to walk together. The old man, with the wisdom and caution of experience, and the child, with the freshness of his innocence, would share stories and silences that would fill the air with profound meaning.

They didn't know where the path would lead

them. They didn't know if there would be mountains or seas, nor if the end would bring joy or weariness. The only certainty was that they had chosen to be launched into this journey called life, which every living being must undertake, and that each step, though uncertain, was necessary.

The afternoon had barely cast shadows over the first steps of the path when the old man and the boy set off together. The old man's well-worn walking stick was a symbol of accumulated experience; the boy, on the other hand, carried only the restlessness of his curiosity, and his restless eyes observed everything, as if it were the first time a rainbow had appeared in the vast sky.

Their union was like that of a river and its course: one brought the memory of all that had been lived, the other the purity of what was just being born. The old man gazed at the earth with gratitude, and the boy looked at the horizon with hope and uncertainty. Thus began the odyssey, both remembering that one does not walk for the sake of walking, but to learn. That life is the path, and that walking is the only way to honor it.

In this way, together, they took their first steps. And without realizing it, the journey had begun.

# CHAPTER II
# THE MAP OF THE PATH

The path grew rockier and the air fresher as dawn broke over the hill. The old man and the boy walked on beneath a gray sky, as the trail forked into several paths. The fresh air and the dew still glistened on the grass like tiny mirrors of crystalline light. The old man walked slightly ahead, as if he knew exactly where they were going. Intrigued, the boy quickened his pace to catch up.

With a restless look, the boy held a crumpled piece of paper in his hands: it was a map drawn with clumsy strokes, without clear routes or an apparent destination. It had no names, no roads, no rivers. Only curved lines, strange shapes, empty spaces, and symbols the boy didn't understand. Mere scribbles to someone who didn't grasp the magnitude of the matter. It was a map, worn by the years and the hands of time.

The boy, interested, asked uncertainly:

What is this paper, Master?

It's the map of the road, the old man replied calmly.

What kind of map is this? he asked.

The only one worth carrying, the old man answered.  A map that doesn't mark destinations… only directions.

The boy looked at a line that seemed to cross the paper like a winding river.

I don't understand, he said.

No one understands it the first time, the old man replied.  And many throw it away because of that.

The boy continued looking at the map.

But… there's no marked end.

Because the end is only discovered by those who walk, the old man said.  Life works the same way. It doesn't tell you where you'll end up. It only gives you clues to help you move forward.

And what does it show, Grandfather? the boy continued.

A map doesn't show the destination, son… it simply shows you how not to get lost. It doesn't tell you where you're going to end up. It only shows you the way to go, the old man replied.

The boy looked at him, confused.

But, Master, why do we need a map if the path is right in front of us? The old man smiled. Because not all paths lead where we want to go, my dear. There are those who walk their whole lives without getting anywhere. And as an old proverb says, he who is going nowhere needs no direction.

The boy was silent, reflecting.

And how do I know if I have direction?

The old man pointed to the map, drawing a line with his finger that disappeared among the mountains.

Direction is born of purpose. Without purpose, the map is just a blank piece of paper, devoid of any meaning. There are people who one day want to climb the mountain, the next want to cross the river, the next want to conquer the world, and the next day they get tired and sit down without having arrived anywhere. They are like travelers without a compass, carried by the wind of their emotions. Like fluctuating children, tossed about by the waves and carried here and there.

The boy, ever observant, turned back and asked:

Who draws the map, Grandfather?

The old man replied calmly:

Usually, the traveler draws the map, but sometimes it's determined by circumstances.

And where do you get it?  the boy inquired.

To which the old man replied: In different places, many times we inherit it from our parents or ancestors, we develop it ourselves, we copy it from someone, and other times, circumstances, difficult journeys, and misfortunes.

Master, the boy asked, how will we know where to go if the map doesn't show the end? The old man smiled, leaning on his cane.  The map isn't made to show you the end, but to remind you that you must have a direction. Whoever wishes to arrive, even without knowing the exact point, needs to plan each step.

The boy gazed at the horizon, hesitating. And what if I make a mistake? What if I choose wrong?

Then you will learn, as we all learn, the old man replied serenely. Mistakes are also part of the journey. Not all steps are perfect. Sometimes we step on the wrong foot. Always remember that one step doesn't take you to your final destination, but it moves you from where you are.

The boy sat beside him and observed the marked paths.

So…do we have to plan every step? The old man shook his head slowly.

Not every step, but the direction. Not planning, not charting a course, is like walking with your eyes closed. No one who wants to build a tower fails to first calculate whether they have the means to finish it. Whether they have the stones, the time, and the strength to complete it. Likewise, no one who wants to achieve a dream can move forward without a clear idea of what they seek. That's how life is: those who don't plan get lost. The map doesn't prevent stumbles, but it shows you where to return when you encounter them.

The boy thought for a moment and said:

So…does the true path have no destination?

The old man smiled.

It has many. But only one will be yours.

The boy smiled, too, and with a stick began to draw his own map in the dirt, comically and as a form of practice.

So, teacher, should I make mine too?

Yes, son, replied the old man, with a slight smile.  Draw your map with dreams, but also with prudence. Mark your goals, but leave room for contingencies, because the path has its own rhythm. Without purpose, every path becomes wearisome. The old man continued:

Life is identical to this journey. There are those who begin with enthusiasm, but without direction; they stray, they tire, and they end up getting lost. And there are those who chart their course, but they don't accept that the winds change, that rivers overflow, that the terrain won't always be flat. They, too, become frustrated. The wise person understands that the map is a guide, not a prison. We must adapt, but never walk without a compass. The journey of life is about a series of adjustments.

And what if I lose the map, Master?  The boy asked softly.

If you get lost, remember where you were going. Because when the heart has a north star, the feet always find the way.  Sometimes you have to lose to win. Try to accept that the only thing they can't take from you is what you've experienced. And that the only thing you'll take with you is what you've lived, so start living what you want to take with you.

From today on, I will begin to live all those things that are invisible to the eyes, and that, when combined, fill the soul, the boy replied.

The wind blew strongly, stirring the leaves of the trees. The old man stopped and looked at the boy.

Remember this: whoever doesn't know where they're going, any path will distract them. Don't live distracted, live with purpose. You weren't born to be perfect, but you were born to be happy. And don't wait to be rich to be happy, because happiness is free.

Does the map guarantee we'll walk where there's no suffering, Grandfather?  the boy asked, with an undisguised expression of curiosity on his face.

No one is free from suffering, and we all have an obligation to learn to face it with wisdom and humility, the grandfather agreed. But it's important to keep in mind that suffering humbles the proud, softens the foolish, and melts the hardened silently and consistently. Sometimes we must be hurt to grow. We must fail to know. We must lose to win, because some of life's lessons are best learned through pain. In ancient times, good gold had to be tested by fire to be proven.

The boy slowly agreed, carefully folding the map. With each step, he understood that this piece of paper, more than a drawing, was a reflection of his life. He put the map in his small bag and looked at the old man with eyes full of determination.

So, Master, what's our next step?

The old man smiled and pointed to the horizon.
To walk, my son. But this time, they knew why. And so they continued, under a sky that was beginning to clear, revealing a sliver of light at the end of the path.

The road no longer seemed uncertain, but promising. Because beyond the distance, what mattered was having a direction, a dream, and the courage to move toward it.

# CHAPTER III

# THE PARALLELISM OF THE PATH AND LIFE

The sun was beginning to set, and its last rays painted the edges of the path. The old man walked slowly, resting his staff on the dry earth, while the boy watched the footprints they both left behind.

The air smelled of dust and distance. In that serene silence, the boy spoke:

Master… why do I sometimes feel that this path is so much like life? The old man smiled tenderly, without breaking stride.

Because it is, my son. The path and life are the same journey with different names. One is traveled with the feet… and the other with the soul.

The old man, with a profound gaze, continued:

The path and life are the same. There are stretches where everything is flat, where the air is fresh, and the sun shines brightly. That is the time of youth, when the body is strong, when steps are light, and mountains seem easy to conquer. It is during this time that great things must be accomplished, because that is what the path prepares us for: to learn, to ask questions, to study, to work, to build a home, and to raise children who will later continue the journey.

Before that, when we were just children, we walked holding the hands of others. We depended on those who guided us, just as a traveler depends on the light of a torch they don't carry. Childhood is that initial stretch where we only begin to distinguish the birdsong, to recognize the stones, the thorns, and the flowers along the path.

Then comes adulthood, when the terrain becomes more demanding. It is the time to build, to make firm decisions, to maintain our pace even when the ground becomes rocky. It is there that the traveler's strength is tested, because there is no one left to carry their burden. Each decision opens a new path, and each responsibility is like a backpack that must be carried with patience.

And later, like every traveler, we reach old age. Then the path becomes less clear, filled with slopes, heavy hills, and stones that trip you up. Steps slow, the body no longer responds with the same strength, aches and pains multiply, and what once seemed easy now demands rest. Old age is that final stretch where the wisest course is not to rush, but to contemplate, to remember the journey, to be grateful for the privilege of having reached this point, and to try to teach others what has been learned.

That's life, my son: first we depend, then we build, and finally we rest. Each stage has its purpose, and none are in vain. Youth is for sowing, adulthood for sustaining, and old age for reaping peace. The path teaches us this clearly: it won't always be flat, the sun won't always be shining, but each step, easy or difficult, is part of the same journey.

The boy walked with hurried steps. His curiosity propelled him forward as if the future awaited him around the next bend.

The old man, tired but with the serenity that comes from experience, lagged a little behind, trusting that the little boy would know how to stay the course.

The path forked before them, and the boy, without thinking too much, chose one way. He moved forward enthusiastically, convinced that each step brought him closer to something new. But, after a while, when he looked up, he discovered that he was back in the same place.

The same crooked tree. The same stone is buried in the ground. The same strange silence that seemed to observe everything.

Confused, he chose another path. He walked, he ran, he stumbled. And once again, he returned to the same spot.

The old man caught up with him and, with a gentle smile, said:

Life has a curious way of teaching us. If you don't learn the lesson, you'll face it again and again. The path may change its appearance, but the lesson will be the same.

The boy frowned, exhaling in frustration.

Do you mean that even if I try my best, even if I run without stopping, I can always end up back in the same place?

Exactly, the old man replied. God, life, or the path itself repeats the lessons until the soul understands them. What changes are the settings, but the root is the same.

The boy tried again. A third time, he took a different path, convinced that this time would be different.

However, when he thought he had ventured into the unknown, he found himself once again facing the same crooked tree, the same crossroads, the same beginning.

He collapsed to the ground, defeated.

I can't get out of here, he said, tears welling in his eyes.

The old man knelt beside him and spoke tenderly:

It's not about running faster or looking for a shortcut. It's about learning. As long as you don't understand what this place wants to teach you, you'll always come back here.

The boy, confused, whispered:

And what do I have to learn?

The old man placed his hand on the boy's head. That life isn't about running away or repeating mistakes, but about stopping, looking inside yourself, and understanding. Only when you change on the inside does the path change on the outside.

The boy remained silent. He took a deep breath and, for the first time, didn't run, didn't hurry, didn't look for another way out. He stood still, listening to the murmur of the wind caressing the trees. And it was then that the landscape began to change. The crossroads slowly faded away. The crooked tree disappeared, the stone turned to dust, and before his eyes, a new path opened up, unlike any before.

The old man smiled with satisfaction.

You have learned. The path always waits, but it doesn't forgive distraction: until you heed its teaching, it will make you return again and again.

They walked for a while in silence. The boy, still moved, looked at the old man as if he were just now understanding the mystery of walking.

Why does the path make us repeat the same things?  he asked. The old man replied serenely: Because life does too. There are those who change cities, jobs, or companions, and yet they still encounter the same problems. It's not the place, son, nor the people. It's the lesson they haven't yet learned.

The boy listened attentively, and after a moment added:

Then, if I learn what I must, the path will open.

That's right, said the old man. The path doesn't punish, it teaches. It only repeats what is necessary until the heart understands.

The old man continued in a measured voice, gazing toward the horizon:

Many live trapped in the cycle of repetition. They stumble over the same stone, love in the same misguided way, and trust in the same empty promises. And they believe that time heals, when in reality, it is understanding that heals. This is what we could call: being sincerely mistaken.

The boy lowered his head, thoughtful.

So, is living learning not to repeat?

Not entirely, replied the old man. Living is repeating consciously, without falling into the same errors. It's knowing when to move forward, when to stop, when to persist and not give up, and when to let go.

The path, now clear, seemed brighter. The air smelled of fresh earth, as if the trail itself were celebrating his understanding.

Look closely, boy, the old man continued. Each stretch of the path has its purpose. Some invite you to run, others force you to wait. There are paths that teach you patience and others that teach you courage. But all of them, absolutely all of them, lead you back to yourself.

The boy smiled.

And if I get lost again?

Then remember what you've learned. Close your eyes, listen to your inner voice, and start again. There is no wrong path for those who walk with an open heart and the intention to improve.

Then the boy frowned, thoughtful.

And why is it that some advance so quickly while others fall behind?

Because each person carries a different

burden, the old man replied. Some walk laden with guilt, others filled with pride or fear. And some travel light, because they have learned to forgive, to let go of what they could not change. Life isn't measured by the distance traveled, but by the lightness with which you travel it, and the changes and adjustments you make.

Life and the journey are, in essence, the same path. On one, your feet wear out, and on the other, your very existence. Both require balance, attention, and wisdom. On both, there are tiring climbs, frightening descents, and plains that seem endless. But the most important thing I always say is knowing where you are on the path. Many run when they should be contemplating, and others stop out of fear just as the horizon begins to open up.

Life, like the path, has seasons, and each one has its purpose.

There is a time to walk and a time to rest, a time to sow and a time to reap, a time to receive shelter from others and a time to become shelter for others.

The wise person is not the one who moves the fastest, but the one who understands where they are on the journey and walks accordingly. I often repeat this: many get lost not because the path is difficult, but because they don't know who they are or what stage they're in.

There are young people who walk with the weariness of the elderly, resigned before their time, without dreams, without curiosity, with withered hope. And there are elderly people who, instead of honoring the years they've lived with serenity, seek to repeat the imprudence of their youth, failing to accept that each cycle has its own beauty and lessons.

The path of life is not a competition; it's a process. Sometimes you move forward sharing laughter, other times shedding tears. There are days when life offers you companionship, and others when it offers only silence. But both are necessary, because both voice and silence teach us something about the soul. Those who don't understand where they are on the path walk in circles.

Maturity isn't about years, but about understanding. Maturity isn't about losing youth, but about gaining clarity. It's recognizing that there was a time to run and now there's a time to lead. There was a time to search, and now there is a time to share what has been found. And as the day draws to a close, you will understand that everything was perfectly woven together: every step, every detour, every pause.

Because life like the journey is not about going far, but about arriving with a peaceful soul, knowing that you have lived each stage with awareness, love, and gratitude.

The boy gazed toward the horizon.

And the stones on the path? Are they punishments?

No, my boy, said the old man.

The stones are lessons. If you stumble and fall, they teach you humility. If you move them aside, they teach you compassion. If you use them to build a bridge, they teach you wisdom.

Every obstacle carries a hidden lesson, and whoever understands them moves forward with purposc.

They walked a few meters in silence. A cool breeze stirred the dust around them. The boy spoke again: Sometimes I get tired, teacher. I feel like the path has no end… that I move forward, but I never arrive.

The old man stopped and looked up at the sky, where the first stars were just appearing.

That's life, my son. It's not a destination that awaits us, but a way of walking. The meaning isn't in arriving, but in understanding. He who lives only waiting for the end misses the miracle of each step.

The boy sighed.

So, is living walking?

Living, the old man replied softly, is walking with love, walking with tolerance. It's stopping when another falls, sharing bread, looking back, and not being ashamed of the footprints you've left, because true triumph isn't arriving first, but arriving with your soul intact.

They continued walking, while the wind played with the dry leaves. The old man added: Remember this, my boy: the path doesn't change, what changes is the traveler. Life isn't measured in years, but in awareness. And he who walks with love, even if his steps are slow, always goes further.

The boy smiled, understanding for the first time that the path wasn't just a dirt track... but a reflection of life itself, a mirror for the traveler, where each step is a decision, and each decision, a way of living.

They both continued walking.

The old man, with a slow but firm step.

The boy, with a light heart and attentive eyes, finally understood that the path isn't measured in distance, but in awareness. He felt that the trail beneath his feet was becoming a mirror of his own destiny. And that, just like in life, it's not about running from the hills or the stony ground, but about accepting each stretch with wisdom, because everything has its time, and each stage prepares the soul for the next step.

# CHAPTER IV

# THE TOWER THAT WATCHES OVER THEIR STEPS

At the start of a beautiful day, when the horizon was still full of promise, and the paths seemed endless, the seriousness of their conversations did not diminish their desire to continue.

Their steps left barely visible footprints on the earth, as if the path itself wished to keep them secret. The silence between them was tranquil, like a pause where each listened to the heartbeat of their own life.

They had already traveled a good distance, but as they approached a unique, almost unbelievable place, they had no choice but to stop. Suddenly, the old man and the boy found themselves facing a tower that stood alone in the morning mist.

In the very center of the path, at a distance precisely measured by millimeters along its diameter, this great tower stood like a giant, serving as a guide, a lighthouse for a ship sailing on the high seas. Its presence was majestic, silent, and the air surrounding it seemed to hold a secret that could only be revealed to those who walked with open hearts. Majestic and silent, adorned with symbols that seemed as ancient as time itself. The origin of its construction, the reason why, or how it came to be there was never known, but they felt it had always been on the path, waiting for them.

Its peak, from any angle, contrasted with the sun, and at night it lay in the path of the moon's clear light. In times of rain, it seemed as if the clouds kissed its summit, and from it emanated a torrent of crystalline water droplets, which could be mistaken for the most exquisite white diamonds of colonial Africa. A rocky wall embellished its side, transforming it into a kind of walled city. It had no guards, like the ancient cities of refuge. The well-crafted fence had no gates; therefore, access to the interior of its courtyards was easy through a space, seemingly left intentionally.

The vast majority of pilgrims paused along their journey, whether out of necessity or curiosity, to contemplate the uniqueness of that place. The interior of the tower was inaccessible, and its entrance door indecipherable, so much so that many, upon entering the garden, raised their eyes to the heavens, circled it, and, with various comments, continued on their way.

Its location made it impossible to miss. Erect against the sky, and so tall that it seemed to touch the firmament. Undoubtedly, whoever conceived it intended it to be an experience within the process or journey. Generally, in the minutes, hours, and seconds following the pause, the topic of conversation was the place, if they were accompanied, and meditation if they were alone.

Everyone agreed that the place was a kind of work of art, somewhat magical, mystical, and perhaps mysterious…? Why not?

It boasted a garden of wildflowers, as if someone were meticulously tending them. Many attested to its healing powers, which they had witnessed firsthand. Having been healed of both mental and physical ailments was explained by the informal shrine of offerings of gratitude attached to one side of the wall. At the foot of the tower, travelers left flowers, stones, or simple gestures of gratitude.

Master, the boy asked, What does this tower mean? Why does it stand like this, as if watching us?

The old man looked at him calmly, his eyes

shining with the memory of past experiences.

This tower, my son, is not a place. It is a mirror of the soul. It is the height to which we must look to discover what we are and what we have been. And the hollow you see at its summit… it is not a hollow that looks and judges, but a point of reference that reminds us of our conscience, the inner voice that always accompanies us, even when the path becomes difficult.

And why do they leave things here? The boy asked curiously.

Because walking is a gift, the old man replied. And those who reach this tower are grateful to be alive, grateful for the steps they can still take, the eyes with which they can still see the path, and the company with which they can enjoy it. The present, as its name indicates, is a gift, and therefore we must consider it as such.

The boy walked around the base of the tower, touching the cold stone and feeling the weight of the years that had formed it. He strolled through its courtyards and flowery surroundings, observing in detail, with that gaze that discovers what others would overlook.

So, master, he asked, what should we learn from it?

We will learn that silence has its own language, the old man replied. That wisdom is not found in shouting voices, but in the stillness that allows us to listen to our inner selves. And that observing the tower does not mean physically ascending, but rather understanding, contemplating, and recognizing the truth that already lives within us.

Grandpa, do you think there's someone up there? Curiously, the boy asked, with the excitement of someone who has discovered a mystery.

There is always someone watching us from above, the old man said. Not only our steps, but what we sow as we walk, and what we say as we go.

The silent tower seemed to observe them from above, as if reminding them that in life there are always invisible eyes watching us: the eyes of conscience, of memory, of the sacred. Every step, every act, leaves a mark not only in the dust of the path, but in what transcends us.

Is someone really watching us? The little boy whispered.

The old man clasped his arms to his chest.

I don't know. Perhaps it is the sky, perhaps life itself. But what is important is not who is watching, but remembering that we do not walk alone. There is always an invisible gaze that accompanies us.

The wind blew softly, raising small clouds of dust around their feet. The boy took a deep breath, feeling an unfamiliar calm, and understood that this encounter with the tower was the beginning of something greater than himself.

Remember, son, said the old man as they moved away from the threshold, that greatness is not always measured by the height reached, but by the clarity with which one observes from silence.

As a token of gratitude for the privilege of walking, the boy and the old man, in the midst of their conversation, also left their offering: a child's drawing and a withered branch gathered at the foot of a wild tree, part of the native flora of the place.

As they continued on their way, they had to pause their conversation for a moment, their breathing becoming ragged. They debated whether to accept the shiver and fervor that permeated the place.

But what they both agreed on, unanimously, was that it seemed as if someone was undoubtedly watching from the summit, and that as they moved away, it was as if their strength had been renewed. And so they continued on their way, with the tower left behind, but with its message engraved in their hearts: a reminder that true vision always begins within.

# CHAPTER V

# THE VALLEY OF DRY BONES AND THE ECHO OF LOST EFFORT

The boy and the old man continued onward. The path, which had previously been firm and bright, began to descend slowly until it opened into a strange, silent valley, shrouded in a light mist that seemed to hold secrets.

They both fixed their gaze on a tree trunk buried at the side of the path. It appeared to be an ancient tree, which the last tornado in the area had shattered. And just behind that gigantic trunk, and the rest of the undergrowth, bones could be found scattered all around. Some were half-buried, others exposed to the elements, as if they rested beside the crosses that proudly adorned it.

It didn't take much intelligence to conclude that the place was a cemetery for beings who had once been part of the path. The representation of the deceased was vast. Bones lay everywhere, of all ages, sizes, possibly ethnicities, and certainly skin colors.

The cause of death was decipherable in this valley of dry bones, and by simple inspection and the sheer size of the place, a wide array of ailments was evident, among which the most prominent were: old age, dehydration, heart failure, suicide, bleeding, and infections of every kind.

There, before his eyes, lay a nameless cemetery. It wasn't an orderly place, the cemeteries' men knew, but an immense valley where bones and lifeless bodies from all eras rested.

It was a sea of fragility exposed to the sun and wind: small and large remains, dark and light, ancient and recent, mingled together as if they all, in the end, shared the same fate.

A fear emanated from among the bones. A feeling one only experience once in a lifetime. The boy shuddered.

What is this place?

The old man lowered his gaze.

It is a reminder of what we are. Here rest

those who walked before us. Some reached the end of their years, others were stopped by illness, and many never even knew why death found them along the way. Such is life: uncertain, fragile, unpredictable.

Here rest those who no longer walk the path? he asked, his voice trembling.

The old man nodded.

Yes…but to rest does not mean to disappear. They walked before us, and every trace they left lives on in those of us who remember them.

The boy crouched beside a moss-covered grave. A small violet flower had sprouted among the cracks in the stone. He gently stroked it and kissed it.

So…is it like this flower?  hc said. Something new is born from the old. The old man smiled, surprised by the clarity of that answer.
Exactly. Life never stops. It only changes form.

In a few moments, the boy, innocently, bent down and picked up a small bone, perhaps from someone who never grew up.

He held it silently, understanding without words that life doesn't guarantee old age, strength, or a future.

Do we all end up here? he asked, his voice hesitant.

Everyone, the old man replied solemnly. It doesn't matter our age, our resources, our race, or where we come from. We are all made of dust, and to dust we shall return. The only things that change are time and form, but the end is the same.

A wind swept through the valley, and the bones rattled against each other, as if complaining or telling forgotten stories. It was a strange murmur, like a chorus of warnings and allusions.

The old man took the boy's hand and led him among the remains, walking with reverence.

This valley teaches us something important: life is fragile, and we must walk with care. Every decision, every step, can bring us closer to or further from this end.

The boy looked at him with frightened eyes.

What if I die soon, too?

The old man gently stroked his head.

We can all die at any moment, but what matters isn't how long we live, but how we walk while we are alive. Fear is also part of life's equation. Always remember that when you live your life in fear, you are only living half your life.

The boy remained silent, holding the weight of that truth in his heart. And as they left the valley, he understood that the cemetery wasn't there to frighten, but to teach and instruct: life shouldn't be taken for granted, because every moment is a gift.

The sun continued its slow descent, gradually warming the edges of the path. The old man and the boy continued their walk for a long time, steadily but without haste, enveloped by the murmur of the wind that rustled through the trees. In the distance, a bird circled the blazing sky, as if searching for a direction that didn't exist.

The boy broke the silence:

Master… Have you ever known someone who thought they had found their destiny, only to discover in the end that they had merely been used?

The old man looked at him gently and nodded:

Yes, son. I knew a man who, from a young age, believed he had found the meaning of his life in his work. He thought that constant effort was the key to fulfillment. And he worked... he worked tirelessly, as if time had no end. He worked as if work were his only option, or as if he were going to live forever.

His days were filled with routines, and his nights with weariness. Each sunrise stole a little of his life, and he gladly surrendered it, convinced that this sacrifice would give him a more secure tomorrow. He didn't take vacations, he didn't celebrate simple moments, he didn't stop to look at the sky. He saved money, but he forgot to save memories. He forgot to create new ones. He made work his defense mechanism and his excuse for not facing other challenges in life.

The boy listened with wide eyes, almost fearing the conclusion, and looking in his memory, as if it were a mystery film, at the cemetery he had just passed. And what happened to him, teacher?

The old man sighed deeply. When his strength began to wane, when his steps were no longer so firm and his hands trembled, when his productive capacity diminished, the system he had served simply cast him aside. They simply replaced him with someone younger and cheaper. They gave him a letter, a certificate of recognition, an empty smile, and a prolonged silence. All that he had become was a forgotten file in a dusty drawer.

The old man stopped. He looked at the horizon and said in a low voice:

Man realized, in the end, that he had been going around in circles, believing he was moving forward. That he had wasted the most precious years of his life giving his best to something that never had a soul. That he had truly plowed the sea and ended up in a torn bag.

The boy lowered his gaze and said:

So, working so much was his mistake?

To which the old man shook his head and replied:

No, son. The mistake wasn't working, but forgetting what one works for.

Work dignifies human beings. Work is noble

when it builds life, but it becomes a chain when it steals the soul. There is no virtue in effort that destroys the one who offers it. Always remember, my son, that we don't live to work, but rather we work to live.

They walked another good distance in silence. Each one pondering thoughts in his own mind, while the afternoon grew more mature, as if the sky wanted to preserve the moment, and as if the silence were an accomplice to them both.

The old man continued:

A man must sow with his hands, but also with his heart. Because the fruit of labor is not in what is earned, but in what is experienced while sowing. Effort without purpose is like walking without direction: one moves forward, yes, but nowhere.

The boy looked at him tenderly and asked:

Master... How will I know if my effort has meaning? The old man smiled, and his voice became almost a whisper:

You will know when your work brings you closer to love, to peace, to satisfaction, and to yourself. He who strives with soul finds rest even in fatigue. But he who sells himself to the system and forgets his essence will one day awaken empty, with his hands full of nothing. With one hand in front and the other behind.

The breeze blew gently, raising the dust from the path. The old man looked toward the sunset and concluded:

Remember this, my son: life does not reward the one who tires the most, but the one who knows how to love the most in the midst of weariness. Because true success is not in going far... but in arriving with your soul intact, you must work, but you must do it intelligently.

The valley was left behind, but the image of the dry bones remained etched on them like an eternal warning: everything that walks will one day stop.

# CHAPTER VI
# THE MOUNTAINS

After weeks of travel, the boy and the old man had faced countless challenges and adventures. Some they took lightly, others bravely, as circumstances demanded. But none compared to what now lay before them. And nothing prepared them for what they would find next.

After descending a rocky slope of almost half a kilometer, among boulders and marshy ground, they reached a small plain where the vegetation parted as if nature itself wished to reveal a secret. There, before their eyes, rose two majestic mountains, tall, imposing, almost twins. Divided by a natural, dark passage that cut through the dense forest like a deep wound in the earth's breast. The sight was so awe-inspiring that for a moment they both remained silent.

The old man, panting, gazed in astonishment.

Am I delirious? he said, wiping the sweat from his face. I think exhaustion has dulled our vision.

Do you mean the mountains or the passage? The boy asked curiously.

Neither, the old man replied, his gaze fixed and profound.  I mean, what's moving beneath the trees.

The boy, confused, exclaimed:

Then clear my mind, because I don't understand anything.

The old man narrowed his eyes and pointed toward the mountainside.

Don't you see movement beneath those trees? If my eyes don't deceive me, it looks like someone is lying in the grass.

Someone?  said the boy.  There's definitely more than one!

Approaching cautiously, they discovered a small group of travelers resting by the entrance to the passage. Their faces showed weariness, but also a mixture of fear and hope. They were discussing how to cross the narrow gorge.

Do you think they've noticed we're here?  The

boy asked somewhat fearfully.

I don't know that, the old man replied.

They tried to get his attention by waving their hands, but no one responded. Then the old man, more afraid than ashamed, exclaimed loudly:

We come in peace!

The tension immediately dissipated. The group's faces relaxed, and smiles began to bloom.

The travelers responded with relief. Soon they joined in a cautious discussion, where they all acknowledged the same thing: that tunnel represented their only passage to the other side of the valley, but no one dared to cross it.

One of them explained:

We arrived at sunset, and seeing how deep the darkness was, we decided to wait until dawn.

The old man nodded.

It was a wise decision. Darkness always confuses those who lack direction. He also prudently observed the entrance to the passageway and added:

It was best not to proceed. That cave looks dark and unpredictable.

I don't think it's a cave, one replied.

Then what would you call it?  The curious boy asked.

Perhaps you're right, another responded, but to me it looks like a tunnel.

Whatever the case may be, said the old man, the important thing is that it has an exit on the other side.

And if it doesn't?  The boy asked.  What if the path ends here? The old man smiled serenely:

Then our lives will have ended in the same place, at the same time, and in the same way. A traveler, who until that moment had remained silent, spoke firmly:

I'm sure there's a way out. And that this isn't the end.

And how do you know that?  another asked suspiciously.

Because I have faith! The young man replied in a strong voice.

Faith...? one replied incredulously. Many confuse faith with a lack of doubt.

Faith, the man said calmly, isn't in what's visible, but in what you perceive within yourself. That's why you can close your eyes and see beyond fear. Faith is the beacon that allows us to move forward even when the path is shrouded in shadow. That's why one can believe even without seeing. Close your eyes, and you'll see that you can travel back to the most important moments of your life, even if they aren't in front of you. Faith allows you to feel the invisible.

We can't be like the bull fighting with the cape when our real enemy is the bullfighter. Visible obstacles aren't always the true dangers; sometimes, what holds us back the most is within ourselves. The mountains teach us that: to believe without seeing the summit. To climb without knowing how much further. To cross without knowing what lies on the other side. To face the darkness, hoping to find light. Faith is the map that guides the soul when the path is invisible.

The group fell silent. Then, the one who

seemed to be the leader stood up and, with a serene, humorous tone, remarked:

Don't try to explain so much... people only see and hear what they want.

Laughter broke the weight of fear, and that night they rested under the stars, preparing themselves to cross at dawn.

With the first rays of sunlight, the old man stretched slowly and looked at the young leader of the group, who was observing the tunnel with determination.

How has the journey treated you so far? The old man asked.

It's hard to explain, the young man replied. Each step brings a different lesson. Everyone has their own experience. No one can walk in another's shoes. Sometimes we carry others, but the time comes when each of us must move forward on our own.

I'm not just referring to you, but to the group in general, the old man said. The young man smiled somewhat arrogantly: Everyone has to make their own effort. In my case, I'm still young and don't need anyone.

That's a good point, the old man agreed. But beware of self-sufficiency, my son. At that moment, the old man looked at him patiently and added:

Youth is treacherous. Sometimes it makes us self-sufficient, and that's dangerous. Wanting to know everything isn't wisdom; it's pride.

And what's wrong with wanting to know everything? The young man persisted.

Wisdom, the old man replied, consists of knowing the limits of knowledge, not in accumulating it, but in applying it purposefully.

The young man raised his eyebrows and, still defiant, said:

I didn't come here to see what will happen; I came here to make something happen.

And that's fine, the old man replied, as long as you do it with conviction. Remember: many live by preferences, not by principles. But mountains are only conquered with conviction.

The group listened in silence. One of the men commented:

He who isn't going anywhere doesn't need direction. The old man smiled, repeating the proverb thoughtfully: Yes… but he who has a purpose, even if the path is uncertain, will always find the light to move forward.

The young leader replied firmly:

Haven't you heard the saying that it's better to walk alone than in bad company?

Perhaps, the old man said, but the truly wise person doesn't walk alone; he shares the path. It does you no good to be satisfied if you can't share that satisfaction with others. Inspiration comes from those who build bridges, not from those who raise walls. Those who argue seek to impose their will; those who communicate seek to understand.

Silence returned for a moment, broken only by the murmur of the wind among the rocks.

The old man continued in a soft voice:

Life is a rollercoaster, and circumstances come and go. Learn from the rabbit, which hides among the rocks in moments of fear. Likewise, man must take refuge in prudence. There are seasons in life as in the year: light and darkness, sun and shade, war and peace. Sometimes, no one can help you, and that is when you must learn the most about yourself.

The entire group pondered these words.

Do not judge anyone by the moment they are living, the old man added. The young may lack experience, and the old may err because of their age. But both are necessary for the balance of the journey.

As they spoke, the sun illuminated the mountaintops.

Do you know why mountains are so high? The old man asked the boy.

Perhaps because they want to touch the sky, the boy replied.

Yes, perhaps, the old man smiled. But also because they rise again and again after each thrust of the earth. Their height is the result of their wounds. So too does the soul rise, not out of pride, but out of resilience.

The wind blew strongly, filling the air with a sense of nature.

In life, my son, some flee from the

mountains because they are afraid to climb. But true rewards are not found in the valleys where everything is easy, but on the summits where silence compels one to listen to oneself.

The old man placed his hand on the boy's shoulder:

Never fear heights. Fear complacency. Because while some complain about the burden of the ascent, others are already gazing at the horizon from above.

Silence once again filled the valley. Before them, the tunnel resembled a sleeping monster, an open mouth daring them to enter. The old man, in a measured voice, concluded:

Mountains aren't always climbed; sometimes they're traversed, as in this instance. And that dark passage is necessary to find the light on the other side. Life docsn't always ask us to climb; sometimes it asks us to pass through fear. To face the unknown. To illuminate, with our courage, the darkness we confront.

The group looked at one another.

The boy squeezed the old man's hand, and

together they took the first step into the passageway.

As they ventured deeper, the echo of their footsteps resonated in the darkness like an eternal reminder: that faith doesn't eliminate fear, but it passes through it.

# CHAPTER VII
# THE WOODCUTTER

Dawn arrived with a gentle clarity, as if the sky wanted to remind the world that each day is a new opportunity to begin again. The boy and the old man walked together, breathing the fresh air that smelled of earth and hope. But, as they covered a stretch of the path, suddenly the sky began to turn gray. And the scattered white clouds, like cotton balls, that adorned the vast blue sky, disappeared in fractions of a second. Then, a torrent of clean water, as clean as the mind of a newborn, flooded the air.

It seemed as if nature were turning all its fury against that piece of land. The trees tried to hide behind themselves. The roots cried out for mercy, the leaves for clemency, and the rain fell so hard, and the wind moved so fast, that it combed the surprised leaves that could barely survive clinging to their trunks. There was no place untouched by the harsh weather, and more and more the local wildlife fled in terror from the habitat they thought they knew.

They were not spared, their faces drenched by the colorless liquid falling from above, and their bodies covered in the mud that had formed among the undergrowth. They found a small shelter that could barely accommodate a few people, and even then, very uncomfortably. Sheltered by dry, badly deteriorated palm fronds, it was of minimal use.

It seemed to be a seldom-visited spot, but judging by the three stones on the ground aligned in a triangle and the remnants of ash, someone had used it not long before. Nevertheless, fearing thunder and lightning, they decided to camp there. There wasn't much to do other than find something to talk about to pass the time. They discussed topics that went beyond the material and the everyday. They engaged in a long conversation, focusing more on the spiritual than the mundane. Each point and hypothesis was made with fervor and such conviction that it was reflected on their faces.

It was almost midday, and after a few hours, the rain stopped. The ground dripped water of every color and flavor, and birds began to take flight everywhere. Their song was like acoustic therapy, infusing sweet melody and the breath of life into existence. The trees of the place spoke of the grandeur of Mother Earth and of humankind's courage and capacity to reinvent itself in times of need, and to make the concept of ideas the instrument and force that moves the world.

As they resumed their journey, the sun peeked out shyly, illuminating the damp earth with its warm light. In the distance, they heard the crack of an axe and the birds singing as the sun set. So far along the path, there had been very little human interaction. Their experiences had become purely naturalistic, and their conversations a buffet for two.

The old man and the boy were walking along the path when they saw a strong, silent man chopping wood by a stream.

The old man stopped and said:

Look, boy. He doesn't speak, but his whole life speaks for him.

The man lifted each log carefully, as if with each stroke he were returning a part of himself to the earth. He didn't seem to work for wealth or glory, but out of necessity and purpose. His gaze wasn't lost in the heavens or in dreams, but in the present moment: in each piece of wood he split, in each drop of sweat that fell to the ground.

The boy asked:

Why does he work so hard if he doesn't seem to be in any hurry, and no one is paying him? The old man smiled.

Because he doesn't work for the world, but for himself. He is the architect of his own destiny. Every day he sows effort, and his harvest is the peace he feels at dusk.

They quickened their pace, filled with curiosity, and went to meet him.

When they stood before the villager, trying to strike up a conversation, the old man asked:

How's your day going, friend?

I'd say productive, he replied with a smile, his tool of the trade, the lumberjack, slung over his shoulder.

Well, I suppose it's a good day, the old man agreed, while the boy watched him.

Not every day is good, he said, but every day you can do something good.

And what brings you to this place, good sir? The old man inquired.

You could say I'm from here, the woodcutter

answered.

From the confidence and composure he displayed, it could be deduced that he knew the area well. A thick beard, abundant gray hair, which he tried to hide beneath a battered straw hat. His face was hard to look at, but his heart was as noble and loving as a harmless cricket on the roadside. A man overflowing with wisdom and experience. Every swing of the axe, every tree planted and felled, every step he took within the area, represented the passion of work done with love and dedication.

The woodcutter had an ineffable gift. He had planted various species of plants along the roadside. Each one had grown successfully, and the most robust provided shelter and shade for the local birds and the often weary passersby on sunny days. Their types and species could be distinguished, meticulously aligned along long stretches of the road. Many others were planted further inland, contributing over the years to what had become a large forest. His hands were prodigious, and the fruit of his labor nourished the bountiful soil, which proudly displayed the majesty of the place.

His raspy voice contrasted with the gentleness of his words. His positivity and dynamism far surpassed the appearance of his face, weathered by the years. When he ventured deep into the forest, the trees trembled with fear. This could be the day the merciless axe would pierce their hearts and turn them into mere firewood. The forester only cut down trees deep in the forest, so those closest to the edge swayed fearlessly in the gentle breeze. They knew their days would not be shortened, barring some unforeseen circumstance. They were the backbone of the path, and the essential element for the passage through the place.

The boy watched him silently, trying to read his mind and anticipate his actions. Suddenly, he broke the silence and asked:

Do you mean you control the entire forest, sir?

What do you mean, little one?  asked the woodcutter.

You can do whatever you want without having to answer to anyone, said the boy. The woodcutter explained: Not necessarily. Free will doesn't mean doing whatever you want. It means having the freedom to do what is right.

Don't you get tired of always being here? asked the boy. To which he replied: I live one day at a time… the present is already a beautiful reason to be grateful, to live, to smile, to appreciate, and to be happy. Besides, I understand that life is made up of days that mean nothing, but moments that mean everything.

And do you like what you do, good sir? asked the boy.

In the end, true happiness is time, health, good company, a peaceful mind, and the freedom to choose what you want to do, said the villager.

The young man looked at him intently and asked:

Don't you ever feel lonely, sir?

The greatest loneliness isn't being accompanied or surrounded by people; it's simply not being at ease with yourself. Without hesitating, the answer was on the tip of his tongue.

Almost before he could finish, the boy asked:

And what are the people like who pass by here? To which he added: I've seen all kinds of people and all kinds of attitudes on this road: good deeds, and behaviors that aren't flattering.

The boy smiled and pressed on with questions:

And do you know where the people who pass by here come from and where they're going? Do they all reach their destination, or do some turn back? Do they ask for help?

The woodcutter replied, elaborating on his answer:

I almost never pay attention to their origins, since we're not to blame for where we come from, but we are to blame for where we're going.

Who hasn't been cheered up in difficult times, their nostalgia and joys stirred by something or someone?

When we let the less important things dictate our lives, we become people with ears but no hearing. Physical beings with fanciful eyes but no sight.

And is it easy to reach the end of the road, sir? Do you know anyone who has?  The boy persisted.

The man replied:

The only thing I could add, my son, is don't lose your dreams, don't give up on life. Remember that triumph goes to the favorite, but victory is achieved by those who strive; those who value the combination of dreams and realities. Smile and lighten the load of life. Don't look at the future with your head in the sand. Don't be one of those who think that living is a crazy task, since we all have a little of that in us, and that when it's not done their way, then it's a failure.

He continued, adding: Don't waste your time on abstractions or chimeras that vanish with time. Harness your dreams and weave your reality, for great things are made of small details.

The old man nodded, and the boy looked at him with a newfound understanding. In that simple man lay a lesson deeper than a thousand words: the greatness of a human being lies not in what they obtain, but in the dignity with which they forge their path.

One last question before we go, the boy exclaimed.

Do you think there are more good people than bad on this path? The old man smiled and said:

Well, in this labyrinth of deceit and falsehoods, I wouldn't bet my grandmother's jewels…

As the sun began to set, the old man and the boy said their goodbyes. As they walked away, the boy turned once more; the woodcutter was still there, chopping wood, as if with each blow he were marking the pulse of the world.

The old man murmured as they walked on:

He who understands the value of effort has already conquered half the journey.

# CHAPTER VIII
# THE MAGIC HOLE

The boy gazed at the horizon with eyes full of wonder, while the old man walked beside him with serene, heavy steps. The wind blew among the stones, and the echo of their footsteps seemed to answer them with ancient voices.

The path stretched out like an infinite line, inviting them to travel it without haste, as if each stone and each shadow hid a secret waiting to be discovered. The boy wanted to run, but the old man calmly stopped him, reminding them that what mattered was not arriving quickly, but learning from each step, for the path was life itself unfolding before them.

At one end of the path, not far from its edge, a narrow passage could barely be seen, covered in leaves everywhere, filling the place with mystery. Seeing the eagerness and prying of that curious boy, the old man had no choice but to quicken his pace.

I think this stretch of the path offers the best opportunity for exploration, the old man said, pointing with his right index finger toward the turnoff.

What do you mean by that?  The boy asked.

You'll see, the old man replied.

They went down and up again, carefully avoiding the occasional obstacle, until they were deep in the sparse vegetation. About two hundred meters away, roughly the length of two city blocks, the boy saw something strange: a small hole in the ground from which a faint bluish light emerged.

The hole was like a kind of bionic eye, through which one could see fears, anxieties, and much more.

What is that?  The boy asked curiously.

The old man bent down, observing cautiously.

They say this is the magic hole of the path. It's like a kind of magical realism. Some say that whoever looks within sees their destiny… others, that they see their fears and anxieties.

The old man peered in first, and upon observing, he could see nothing but mists, fogs, and a poorly constructed bridge held up by the dew of darkness. This scene reflected his stage as a human being. His best years were behind him, but the uncertainty of the unknown and infinite filled him with a touch of fear.

With nothing more to add, he took two steps back and gave the boy, who was dying, his chance.

The boy approached and, without thinking, peered out.

At first, he saw nothing, only darkness. But soon the light began to change… I don't know why the sun shines so brightly, the boy said, almost as a question.

Lucky you that you can see it! replied the old man.

But the moon also shines beside it, the boy continued.

Are they together? The old man asked, simply out of curiosity.

In his vigorous and creative mind, the boy began to paint a world of fantasies and imaginings.

I don't know how long they've been friends. The old man played along:

As long as there's room for both of them, I don't see it as a problem. Besides, don't worry about them; worry about those who are watching them. He meant that in life, there is always room for coexistence despite differences. When there is a shared vision of destiny, it is possible to overcome disparity. And specifying that when you have an idea, you must work on it regardless of public opinion. Also, for some people, it doesn't matter what you do, because regardless of how you behave in their eyes, you are already disqualified. Your commitment is not based on what others think of you, but on what you think of yourself and what you do, since that is the only thing you can control.

This was a wonderful scene. A child's creativity made the impossible possible. Two celestial bodies so different and with such distinct characteristics; in his mind, he could see them together. His vitality and zest for life could make the sun shine like never before. He had a whole life ahead of him, without limits. He had time and space to create and uncreate, to err and correct, to walk, run, and fly.

This child only wanted to see positivity. His

desire to explore a world of colors, dreams, and possibilities was immense.

Suddenly, his tone of voice changed, and he exclaimed:

All those people haven't even noticed that the sun and the moon, despite their great size, are there together. I think they're too busy with their own trivialities and petty concerns to dedicate time to these details.

He wanted everyone to share their dreams. It's as if he had traveled to the future and realized that our ideas aren't always well-received, that not everyone sees things from the same perspective as we do. People often discard what is good and opt for what is mediocre. Those who possess the truth must remain silent so as not to offend those who lie. And that is what means nothing to some is more than enough for others.

After this, he looked again, and images appeared within the hole: places he had dreamed of, people he had loved, and also moments he wished he could forget. He saw time swirling inside, mixing memories, illusions, and fears. His heart raced. He took a step back.

I don't want to look anymore! he cried. That can't be real!

The old man took him by the shoulder.

Everything you've seen is real in your mind, and that's why it has power over you. But the hole doesn't show the future or the past… it shows the soul of the one who dares to look.

The boy lowered his head, still trembling.

So… there's no magic?

The old man smiled gently.

There is. But it's not in the hole, but in the one who faces it without running away.

The ancient man couldn't hide his admiration for the skill and curiosity of such an innocent creature.

The old man looked inside again, and for a moment his eyes filled with tears. He said nothing. He closed the hole with a stone and continued on his way to the main road.

The boy walked beside him in silence,

understanding that he had seen more than an illusion: he had seen the truth of himself.

When they were far away, the wind blew across the ground, and the hole disappeared, as if it had never been there.

The old man murmured:

The road always has mirrors, but not everyone dares to look at themselves in them.

There was a long silence and then a solemn smile that, without uttering words or sounds, shattered any argument like a jigsaw puzzle breaking piece by piece. The old man whispered: Remember that life is existence within a limited space of time, that matter is not destroyed, that the soul never dies, but the physical body does.

And amid laughter and murmurs, they disappeared into the distance, their figures growing smaller and smaller.

# CHAPTER IX

# THE WOMAN ON THE ROAD

One morning, barely taking flight, more eager to hide than to exist, that wounded bird, which had once been part of a flock, intently observed everything around it. It moved its tail rhythmically and settled itself on its right leg, as if to the rhythm of a ballet, repeating the movements. The bird flew vigorously, vertically upward with a power never before experienced, as if it wanted to say something to its surroundings or as if it were a kind of farewell. From its right wing, a silver feather detached itself and hung suspended for a time, like a pendulum in the air.

The sound of the wind, like ocean waves coming and going, magically brought joy to the abundant forest of gigantic trees and Herculean quantities of leaves that danced among themselves. Some, unable to resist the allure of a strong breeze that blew for three days straight, fell onto the soft, patiently awaiting ground, while others clung to the branches like a frightened child experiencing its first bout of flatulence.

Timid in her gait, drenched in sweat, and with a stomach so empty it seemed she hadn't eaten a bite in a week, the silhouette of that young woman appeared, approaching the path step by step as if she didn't want to be there.

The old man and the child walked in silence when they spotted her in the distance. She walked with slumped shoulders, and her gaze was lost in the earth. Her lips moved, but she didn't seem to be speaking to anyone; it was as if she were reciting a monologue to the wind, as if confessing to the road itself.

She had deep eyes, weary from weeping, but still filled with a serene beauty. And in her monologue, one could deduce a life weary of disappointments and difficult days.

Is it fair to lose my way?  She asked herself.

Perhaps, sometimes we deserve it...  She answered herself.

He failed me...  the young woman murmured.  I believed in what glittered on the outside, in what seemed solid and beautiful... but it left me empty, it left me broken. What good is beauty that fades? What good is brilliance if the heart is empty?

Various voices swirled in her mind, like fish swimming in circles in a small, colorful fishbowl.

Oh! Now I remember the day I decided not to say no!  She burst out, sobbing.

Perhaps this is my punishment, she added.

As she walked forward, unstoppable, she pulled a piece of writing from inside her left bra, closer to her heart and her feelings, and began to recite it as a consolation prize for her misfortune, in the style of great Broadway performers on stage:

"You were the one who dreamed my dreams, and in them I awoke to find you asleep. I traversed possibilities and dodged efforts so as not to see you in your colorful laughter. You departed as lightly toward the unknown as the other seafaring peoples, and you found your new world like a conqueror upon the horizon, and only your memory remains of what you were to others. What a pity and sadness that your legacy in my life is in agony and almost a corpse.

That your ideals, like a song to love in refined prose and poetry, remain in the mirror of oblivion. That you are no longer a reference point for a bastion of dreaming youths who barely reach their first twelve years, but who have already slain many wicked ideas with their cannon of imagination. One day, I believed that to love was to give without measure, that it was enough to give everything to be reciprocated. But I learned that there are loves that blind, that the heart, when it does not listen, gets lost among mirages.

I walked along paths that were not mine, waiting for someone to point me out the right path, until I understood that no one can walk for me the stretch that belongs to me. I have wept for what was and for what will never be, but even with tears in my eyes, I know I am still alive. And as long as the path exists, there will always be a new possibility to begin."

And like a soldier going into battle, who has prepared in theory for the worst, but is overwhelmed by the reality of the unknown, this woman suffers relentlessly. Making a superhuman effort, she struggles to find meaning in the various paragraphs of that classic book of life that everyone had referred to and that she was supposed to understand.

Her words slipped away like stones rolling downhill.

Master, the boy said softly, why does that woman seem so sad? The old man stopped and observed in silence.

Because there are sorrows that weigh more than the weariness of the body he replied.

Let's go closer.

The boy moved, approached her, and asked:

Why do you cry so much on the road?

She looked up and sighed:

Because I let myself be guided only by what my eyes saw. I followed an elegant figure, an attractive face, an appearance that seemed to promise security and love. But inside, there was no truth. Only appearance, only an empty reflection.

I've walked so far, she said without being asked. I gave everything I had, and what little I had left I gave to love. But love also left, like water through my fingers. I was left empty, without the strength to go on.

The old man sat down beside her, respectfully.

The road doesn't only take us forward, he said in a measured voice. Sometimes it forces us to stop to heal.

The woman sighed.

I thought love was a place to stay, not a journey. And when it left, I felt that everything else lost its meaning.

The silence that followed was profound. The old man gazed at her tenderly, aware that at that moment, no words could offer comfort.

The child, his innocence undiminished, took the old man's hand and asked softly:

Can we help her?

The old man sighed. My child, there are paths that can only be traveled alone. Sometimes the soul needs to get lost in order to find itself again. It will know when to move on.

He looked at her gently. Love doesn't go away, he replied. It changes shape, like a river changes when it encounters a rock. But it keeps flowing, even if you can't see it. The heart has the strange habit of being reborn, even when we think it's dead.

She lowered her gaze, and a tear rolled down her cheek.

What if I don't want to love anymore? She asked, her voice breaking. What if I'm afraid?

The old man took a handful of earth in his hands and let it fall slowly.

Fear is also part of love. Only those who have once loved deeply fear. But look at this seed: if it doesn't fall to the ground, it can't bear fruit. That's how the heart is, my child. If it doesn't give itself, it doesn't bloom.

The boy, who had also been listening silently, approached and offered her a small wildflower he had picked from the path.

Here, ma'am. It's small, but it's still alive.

She smiled for the first time in a long time. She stroked the flower tenderly and placed it in her hair.

Perhaps love hasn't completely left, she whispered. Perhaps it has only changed its face.

The old man nodded.

Love doesn't always arrive in the way we expect. Sometimes it comes disguised as friendship, as companionship, as a kind word in the midst of weariness. Other times, like now, it comes in the innocence of a child who reminds you that life goes on. Love, though fragile, is the force that always pushes us to keep walking.

The woman slowly stood up.

I will continue walking, she said. But this time, not waiting for love to find me, but carrying love with me.

The old man listened in silence. He saw in this young woman the fragility of those who mistake the brilliance of the external for the clarity of the internal.

Then you have understood the secret of the path, the old man said, smiling contentedly. As she walked away, the boy asked, Master, do you think she will find love again?

The old man looked toward the horizon, where the woman's figure blended into the light of the setting sun.

Love is never lost, he replied. It only waits for the right moment to bloom again.

From a distance, the old man watched her walk away and said to the boy: Look, son, life knows when to send what we need. Even if circumstances harden your skin, don't let them harden your heart.

The boy nodded, watching the woman disappear into the rays of the sun. The old man rested his cane on the ground, and they continued on their way, knowing that the path doesn't end: it only changes its face.

The woman smiled faintly, grateful for the company that had sustained her in her frailty.

Clearly, weariness was sapping her hope, and in the coming and going of her thoughts, the hours passed like people getting on and off at a train station, while the train continued its course. Reaching the limits of her strength, exhaustion overcame her, and that night she fell asleep by the fire, while the stars watched over her rest.

In that natural universe, on that night, it was impossible to count the stars. So many, like mirrors in a dense forest filled with trees whose leaves were so strange that their shapes were reflected in them.

One after another, with diverse forms like geometric figures or drawings by children just beginning the adventure of holding a pencil for the first time. The moon served as a backdrop, its silhouette reflecting the lost gazes of imaginary celestial souls and undecipherable lives within the spectrum of imagination.

At dawn, the dew bathed the leaves, and a soft birdsong heralded the day's rebirth. The young woman stood ready to begin her journey. She rose, took a deep breath, and with a serene step resumed her walk. With a clear mind, renewed spirits, and amidst the echo of laughter, she understood the solstice of a world of love that begins for some, and the equinox of realities that concludes for others.

Life truly throws you curveballs! She thought. It's like a yo-yo. It goes up, it goes down, and sometimes it even touches the ground. I must stop worrying about what others think of me and start worrying about the concept I have of myself. They tried to sell me the world when the world is truly mine...

With a halting, whispering voice, after a sip of her self-medicating drink, she brushed the dust from her sandals and continued on her way.

Not far away, around a bend in the road, where the breeze was cool and the earth smelled of new life, she encountered another traveler who greeted her with a warm smile. He was a serene man, with a clear gaze and unhurried hands. She recognized him from afar, not by his face, but by the calm he instilled in her.

Their eyes met, and in that simple encounter, the weight of her past began to dissolve. At first, there were no grand words, only a glance that spoke volumes. He wasn't elegant or ostentatious; his gait was simple, his clothes unadorned, but his gaze was steady and his voice sincere. The young woman recognized him instantly: it wasn't the allure of appearances she sought now, but the peace that comes from a true heart.

Then she said:

I understand that my eyes can deceive me, but the heart is never wrong if it learns to listen.

The traveler nodded and added:

In life, woman, what is beautiful is not always true. There are beautiful faces that hide shadows, and humble countenances that hold light. The path teaches us to look beyond what the eyes see, because whoever only looks at the surface walks blind.

She, with her renewed innocence, smiled and said:

Then, what matters is not what is seen, but what is felt and what is given. She raised her head, more upright than before, and understood that her wound was not the end, but a lesson of the path: learning to discern between what dazzles and what truly illuminates.

He offered her a pause, not promises. And she, without knowing why, accepted.

They left the path, entering a clearing surrounded by trees gilded by the light of the setting sun. Their encounter was so magical that they talked for the rest of the day, unaware that night had surprised them.

There, among dead leaves and a gentle breeze, they shared a quiet, profound intimacy, where there was no need to speak of the past. Together, by the warmth of a new fire, they discovered hidden feelings and revealed secrets of intimacy, witnessed only by the fallen leaves and the clear night under the starlight. He touched her as one caresses something one doesn't want to break. She surrendered not as one who forgets, but as one who chooses to remember from a different place.

It was an unhurried encounter, sacred in its simplicity, where the body became a fearless language. Afterward, they rested in silence, side by side, as night fell upon them, hardly noticing.

And so, at dawn, they remained together, understanding that the heart, more than the eyes, is what should guide our steps. And that even if we are not completely healed, sometimes it is enough to just be alive, and to understand that we deserve more than pain.

# CHAPTER X
# WHEN TRUTH IS SOLD

The old man and the boy arrived at a bustling coastal town. Its streets were a mosaic of colors, with fishermen offering their wares, children running barefoot, vendors calling out on street corners, and sailors telling exaggerated tales of distant seas. From the outside, the place seemed like a joyful paradise. But soon, upon closer inspection, they discovered the town's other side. There was everything: hardworking and honest people who struggled every day, mothers devoted to their children, and young people with sincere dreams. But there were also many corrupt individuals, abusive bosses, thieves, and those who lived by deceit.

The boy noticed a group of lying men in particular. They presented themselves as successful: surrounded by women, full of laughter, feigning confidence and success. They had many conquests thanks to their sweet, but hollow, words. And yet, the simple and sincere men went unnoticed, often silent and without the glitter of appearances.

Intrigued, the boy asked the old man: Why do they always seem to win? Why is lying more attractive than the truth?

The old man looked at him and, pointing to the horizon where the sea reflected the sunlight, replied:  Lies dazzle like a reflection on the water; they shine only while the tide sustains them. But when it calms, they disappear. Truth, on the other hand, is like the sun: it's always there, even when clouds sometimes hide it.

The boy and the old man walked through the village and arrived at a plaza where many merchants offered all kinds of products: fruits, fabrics, metals, and even words written on parchment. There was a strange bustle, as if in that market they traded not only things, but ideas themselves.

In a corner, three men shouted:  I sell truths! To the highest bidder!

One was a politician, another a religious figure, and the third was a street vendor. They had settled at a table with a handwritten sign that read: "The forbidden becomes desired."

There were long lines to reach the table where they were sitting, lines that stretched mercilessly throughout the place.

People approached and bought phrases that they tailored to their needs. Some acquired words that justified their mistakes; others paid for softened versions of what they didn't want to hear; and still others didn't even read what they bought. They simply did it because it was part of the routine and daily life of that environment.

The boy, confused, asked:

How can truth be sold? Shouldn't it belong to everyone? The old man replied in a grave voice:

Son, when truth is sold, it ceases to be truth. It becomes merchandise, and merchandise always adapts to the buyer's desires. Authentic truth cannot be bought or accommodated; it is sought, accepted, and often, it hurts.

The boy looked at the merchant, who smiled contentedly at his coins, and understood that lies disguised as truth will always find customers.

Then he asked:

And how do we recognize the truth?

The old man placed his hand on the boy's shoulder:

The problem with these people is that they have been victims of repeated lies that, over time, have become truths in their minds. Truth cannot be bought or sold. It is lived. The just person carries it within, even if the world denies it.

As the days passed, the boy and the old man watched as the masks began to fall. The liars began to suffer the consequences of their deceptions: hurt women who left them, friendships that faded, lives that lost their meaning upon discovering they were built on empty appearances. In contrast, those who remained true to the truth found respect, sincere love, and companionship that didn't depend on illusions.

The old man then added, in a serene but firm tone: This town is like the world. It's full of injustices, of selfish people who only think of themselves, who seek to shine at the expense of others. But there's something that never changes: the sun rises for everyone. It shines on the liar as well as the truthful, the corrupt as well as the honest. The difference lies in how each person receives that light. The selfish person takes it only for themselves, and their shadow betrays them. The humble person, on the other hand, shares it and transforms it into hope.

On life's journey, we don't only find stones, mountains, or rivers to cross. There are more dangerous and invisible obstacles: the influences of power and money. Many men and women begin with firm principles, with a clear moral compass, but discover that being right isn't always enough when economic or social dependence binds them to others. Money, when it becomes the master, slowly erodes dignity. What seemed non-negotiable yesterday is now condoned with complicit silence.

Thus, those who once defended justice end up justifying injustice, and those who preached honesty end up tolerating corruption, because their livelihood depends on the power of others. The problem worsens when those in leadership positions whether politicians, religious leaders, bosses, directors, or institutions live with their backs turned to the truth. When their interests are not affected, when their comfort is assured, they simply choose to ignore what they don't want to see. And in doing so, they drag down those who depend on them.

History repeats itself in every sphere. In political parties, ideals are corrupted when the desire to retain power outweighs the commitment to the people. In religion, faith is distorted when the message is tailored to protect the image or privileges of leaders, forgetting that truth belongs to no one. In social and economic life, morality weakens when what matters is no longer the common good, but personal gain. The old man and the young man, while refreshing themselves in the shade of a sycamore tree, spoke of these things.

The young man, confused, asked:

And what about those who grow strong through injustice? They seem happy, they seem to live better than others.

The old man looked at him calmly and replied:

The unjust may feign happiness, but their soul never rests. They may possess power, riches, or recognition, but deep down, they know they have strayed from the path. On the other hand, the just may lack everything, yet they sleep peacefully and walk lightly, for justice grants them freedom. Listen carefully, young man: the worthy are strong, but the just are happy. And the just never lose their courage, even if the whole world presses upon them.

The young man remained silent, and a spark of understanding ignited in his gaze. He understood that justice was not an ornament of life, but its very foundation, and that defending it was as vital as breathing. The path then becomes a terrain fraught with invisible traps, where travelers who yield to the pressure of the powerful will lose what is most precious: their own dignity. For the truth is that it does not conform to interests, nor does it depend on institutions. Truth is and remains, even if people deny or disguise it.

In the end, what defines a human being's worth is not the money they earn, the party they support, or the temple they frequent. It is the capacity to stand firm, to be just and dignified even when economic, social, or religious factors pull them in another direction. Because whoever loses their dignity, even if they retain wealth or position, has lost the most essential element of the journey: their sense of self. And whoever is unjust may accumulate everything the world offers, but will never know true happiness.

The boy understood that it wasn't a matter of who appeared more virtuous, but of who knew how to walk in the sunlight with a pure heart. Silently, he followed the old man as they walked away from the village, carrying a clear lesson with him: appearances are deceiving but truth always finds its place, because the light reaches everyone, and only the sincere know how to take advantage of it.

The boy treasured those words in his heart, understanding that along the way there would be those who preferred to pay for deception rather than uphold the purity of truth.

Finally, as they walked along a rocky stretch, the old man said forcefully:

Remember, always, that a half-truth is a lie by omission.

# CHAPTER XI
# CASTLES IN THE AIR

Life is a journey where not everything is built with stone and mud; often, we build on the invisible, on what cannot be touched, on what the soul dreams of. These are castles in the air, those born from a memory, a melody, or a scent that transports us back to who we once were.

There are days when a song takes us back to childhood or to a time when our hearts beat differently. At the time, it brought joy, but today it awakens nostalgia because those who were by our side no longer walk with us. That music becomes a bridge between what we lived and what we lost.

The same is true of life's flavors. There was a time when our bodies were healthy and light, and we ate without fear, enjoying the simple things. Now, health sometimes imposes limits, and what was once a feast now becomes a problem, or a distant memory. The athlete who once ran lightly now tires on the hills of the road; The memory that once held every detail now stumbles on the stony ground of oblivion. Faces whose beauty seemed eternal are now adorned with wrinkles and gray hair.

The same is true of the work we once had and perhaps didn't value. We pass by that place and feel an emptiness, as if the echo of what we were was calling to us from within. Mismanaged resources, money wasted, and the prosperity that is now conspicuously absent.

The same happens with the city or town where we were born: its streets are still there, but what we long for is not the walls or the squares, the park benches where we often sat, but the time we spent there, the voices that accompanied us, the faces that are no longer there, the true friends who are gone.

These are moments when life shows us its fragility, its delicate nature. Nothing is eternal; what we believe to be solid today may become swampy ground tomorrow. What seems eternal today becomes a memory tomorrow. But instead of sinking into sadness, these memories invite us to recognize the richness of having lived. And the sadness we feel when looking back is not an enemy; it is a teacher. It teaches us to value what we have while we have it, because every moment is unrepeatable. If something hurts when we remember it, it is because at the time it gave us joy, it gave us strength, it gave us meaning, it gave us courage.

The road became wide and silent. On either side, as if suspended in the mist, fantastical structures began to appear: shining lighthouses, crystal walls, palaces made of light, and bridges of rose petals.

They were so beautiful that they seemed unreal, and in truth, they were: they floated in the air, like untouchable illusions.

The boy stopped, amazed.

Look, old man! Castles!

The old man observed calmly, and in his eyes, nostalgia mingled with melancholy, and joy with sorrow.

Those are castles in the air, he said softly. They represent everything we once had and failed to appreciate. What could have been but never was.

The boy looked at him, confused.

How can someone have something so beautiful and not see it? The old man sighed.

It happens more often than you think. Some people have a loving family and neglect them. Others have a good job, a brilliant opportunity, and let it slip away.

Some people enjoy good health and squander it excessively. At the time, they take it for granted, almost invisible. Only when they lose it do they discover how valuable it was. That's why the saying goes, "You don't know what you've got till it's gone."

The boy frowned and asked:

And can you get it back? The old man shook his head. Not always. Often, when we understand, it's too late. The castle vanishes into thin air and never returns. Sometimes what was and isn't, is as if it never was.

They walked a few more steps, and the old man continued in a grave voice:

In life, we often learn more from defeats than from triumphs. Pain opens the eyes that joy keeps closed.

And the curious thing is that, sometimes, the worst mistakes aren't the ones we make, because at least we learn from those. The worst are the ones we never try: the words we didn't say, the steps we didn't take, the opportunities we let slip by, the loves we didn't declare, the fears we didn't face, and the risks we didn't take. Those are mistakes too, even though we often don't understand them until it's too late.

The boy lowered his gaze.

So, is it possible to make a mistake without doing anything?

Yes, the old man replied. To make a mistake by omission. That mistake is silent, but it leaves deeper wounds than an impulsive act. What's more, do you want to know something? Even the justice system penalizes what is supposed to be done but isn't. These are the famous crimes of omission.

As they spoke, one of the castles in the air began to slowly vanish. The boy watched it sadly, as if something precious were slipping through his fingers.

It vanished like water through my fingers, Grandfather. What if I let my opportunities slip away, too? he asked fearfully.

The old man looked at him intently.

Then you will learn, as we all did. But if you manage to open your eyes in time, perhaps not all your castles will vanish.

You may be able to inhabit some of them, even if only for a moment. And believe me, that moment is worth more than a lifetime dreaming of what could have been. Always remember that you won't live long enough to make all the mistakes in the world and learn from them. This means you must learn from the mistakes of others.

The wind blew hard, and the castles gradually disappeared until the air was clear again. Only the road remained.

The boy took a deep breath and, with a firm step, resumed his walk. He had understood something essential: defeats teach, triumphs deceive, and the greatest mistake is letting life pass him by as if it were eternal.

The true value of castles in the air lies not in their lasting power, but in the fact that they teach us to live gratefully in the present. The past is gone, but it reminds us that we still have time to build new towers, sow new dreams, walk new paths with the same hope, and create new memories.

Thus, castles in the air are not lost illusions, but footprints of the soul that remind us of what is essential: the important thing is not to hold on to everything, but to have lived it to the fullest. Because every memory is proof that we have loved, we have fought, and we still have the strength to continue conquering the pathway.

# CHAPTER XII

# WHEN WE WANT TO LIVE

The sun was beginning to filter through the branches along the path, and the old man, with a slow but steady step, looked at the boy and said:

You know, little one? There are moments on the journey when the soul grows weary, when the steps become heavy, and the horizon seems a line too distant to reach. Then, the traveler wonders if it is worth continuing, if there really is something beyond the hill, or if the journey has been nothing more than a mirage of desire. But when we want to live, something deep inside awakens... and we simply want to live.

The boy looked at him attentively, but didn't say a word. To which the old man continued: It's like a spark that refuses to die, an inner voice that murmurs: "You haven't seen everything yet, you haven't felt all that life can give you."

They had passed through storms and along barren paths, but at that moment, everything seemed to make sense.

Then the boy looked up again, curious.

And what is it to truly live, Master?  he asked innocently.

The old man smiled, like someone who possesses the answer and yet knows it can't be fully expressed.

Sometimes we think life boils down to surviving, but living is when something in the soul ignites, when every step has a meaning that needs no explanation. It's when we laugh without fear, when we love without measure, and when the heart feels at home. Living isn't just breathing, nor maintaining a pulse. Living is having fire in your eyes, purpose in your chest, hope in your wounds.

It's getting up after falling and turning pain into learning. Rubbing your ailments with the balm of optimism, and making your scars painless marks. So that even though they're there, they no longer cause you pain, but serve as reminders of your resilient spirit. When we want to live, every leaf, every ray of sunshine, every word, every drizzle becomes a sign from the universe inviting us to keep walking.

The boy thought for a moment and said:

So, isn't living just about following the path?

No, my boy, the old man replied. Following the path is necessary, but wanting to live is what illuminates it. There are days when we understand that every fall, every silence, every attempt is worthwhile... because in the end, every moment of joy outweighs a thousand sorrows. The traveler who desires to live doesn't fear the storm because he knows that after the rain, the air is purified. After bad weather comes calm, he learns to love even the stones on the path, because in them he sees the footprints of those who walked before him. In them, stumbles, more than blows, become lessons.

He knows that life isn't conquered in great achievements, but in the small acts of courage that push us to take another step, even when the soul trembles, and when spirits flag. And it is then, in that moment of decision, that wanting to live becomes a miracle. Not because life changes, but because our perspective changes. Life is always the same, and it will continue its course; what changes is our perspective. We discovered that life is a gift renewed with each sunrise, and that even suffering has its secret purpose: to remind us that we are alive.

Master, the boy said with a smile, like someone beginning to understand more and more:

Isn't it wonderful when we have the will to live? When our heart beats strongly, and we feel that everything is possible, that the world is full of colors and new paths?

The old man looked at him tenderly and replied:

Yes, little one. It is in those moments that we understand that living is not just about existing, but about having a reason, an inner fire that drives us. To live is to return to our origins, to mature toward childhood, to do and love those things that truly make us happy.

The boy closed his eyes and felt the wind on his face.

Then he understood that it wasn't necessary to reach the end of the road to feel alive. It was enough to look at the sky, hear the river, listen to the birds singing, be grateful for life, and dream…and dream.

How much strength do I need to truly live, as you say, grandfather?

The old man looked at him with compassion, took him in both hands, and said:

Wanting to live is the bravest act of the soul. It doesn't arise from pleasure or comfort, but from the recognition that life, even with its burden of pain and loss, remains a sacred mystery worth inhabiting. Wanting to live doesn't mean ignoring the darkness, but facing it head-on and deciding that even within it there is a spark worth igniting. Holding a lit torch, illuminating the path, even when it is uncertain, is courageous.

Every day we choose to continue, we are defying the void. In that choice lies human greatness: the capacity to transform suffering into strength, need into faith and hope, falling into wisdom, and wounding into compassion. Wanting to live is affirming that existence has meaning, even if we don't always fully understand it. It is trusting that dawn will return, even when the night seems dark and endless.

Grandpa, if I eat well and keep my body healthy, am I living well? The little boy asked in an angelic voice.

To which the old man replied:

I would love to say yes, he said, smiling. Then, raising his face, he added:

But the soul doesn't walk alone; the spirit also needs nourishment. It doesn't matter what you believe in, or what name you give to the mystery that sustains you. The essential thing is to recognize that within you there is a presence that asks to be cared for, a voice that calls you to calm, to faith, to hope. Nourishing the spirit is remembering that there is something greater than ourselves, something that drives us to continue when reason fails. That invisible nourishment prayer, meditation, love, gratitude, helping those in need is the sustenance of the traveler who does not give up.

And when we lose someone we love, Grandfather? When absence becomes a shadow, and the heart seems to crumble, is it natural to feel that the desire to live fades?

My beloved son, the old man replied, when sadness envelops us, when the world loses its color, and our steps become heavy, it is even in that profound pain that we must find a form of respect and reverence that calls us to continue. Living, then, becomes a silent tribute to those who have departed. Moving forward is not forgetting, but honoring their memory with every act of kindness, with every breath of hope, with every day conquered.

When you truly want to live, he continued, it

doesn't matter if your body aches, if illness strikes, or if your strength wanes. Life remains a miracle. Sometimes, fulfillment doesn't consist of reaching the summit, but in learning to smile as we climb. To find the sparkle in life, even in adversity, is an act of wisdom.

Living because you want to and not just out of inertia is the beginning of all transformation. It is the awakening of the being who has understood that life is not measured by years, but by the intensity with which one loves, forgives, and gives thanks. When we truly want to live, we stop merely surviving: we begin to create, to heal, to discover the hidden beauty in the everyday.

Because deep down, wanting to live is an act of love for ourselves, for those around us, and for the very path we have been given to walk. And as long as that deep desire to continue exists, life will always find a way to blossom within us.

After a pause, the old man, looking at the boy who was measuring his steps on the path, said to him in a low, almost inaudible voice:

There is no greater force than the desire to continue. As long as the heart wants to live, the path will always open. Because when we truly want to live, the entire universe conspires to embrace us with life itself. When we want to live, the path ceases to be a climb… and becomes flight.

The boy looked at him, understanding without words.

And so, the sun, bronzed on the distant mountains, seemed to bless their steps, and under the light of dawn, they both continued walking. More united than ever, they continued towards the horizon, with the certainty that living is nothing more than an act of love towards the present.

# CHAPTER XIII

# THE LANGUAGE OF WATER

The boy and the old man walked along the bank of a river that wound its way between silvery stones. The sun, filtering through the branches, played with the reflections on the water, which seemed to speak its own language.

It seems the water has a voice, said the boy, bending down to touch it.

The old man smiled.

Rivers always speak, my son. The problem is that very few people learn to listen to them. The boy looked at him curiously.

And what do they say?

The first thing they do is invite nature. That's why they are always surrounded by trees, fish, and birds that adorn their surroundings.

They also tell us what life tries to tell us at every turn, replied the old man. They speak to us of time, of perseverance, of strength, of the need to keep going, and to reinvent ourselves, even though the paths change. Look how the water doesn't stop at the stones; It surrounds them, caresses them, flirts with them, dances a waltz with them, but continues on its course. It never stops, even if it encounters stones or branches. It doesn't complain, it doesn't give up. It simply seeks its path, with patience, with humility. And although it sometimes appears dirty, its nature returns it to its clarity.

Such must be the soul of the traveler.

The boy observed the currents that flowed harmoniously. So... the river is wise.

Yes, said the old man, because it has learned to accept what it cannot change and to transform itself without losing its essence. It adapts to the environment that contains it. That is what men forget. They want to dominate life, when what they should do is flow with it.

A fish jumped in the middle of the riverbed and broke the silence.

And what if the river gets tired? asked the boy.

The old man looked at him tenderly.

The river doesn't tire, my son. It only transforms. Sometimes it becomes rain, other times mist, and when it falls again, it remains the same. That's how we are: we change form, but not soul. We change scenery, but we continue living.

They walked a long way until, as evening fell, the sound of the water changed. It was no longer a current, but stillness. In the distance, a mirage was slowly transforming into reality: a green strip, a spring emerging from the heart of the desert. Before them, a small oasis shimmered in the light of the setting sun.

The old man stopped.

Look, my son. Just as the river finds rest in the valley, we too need a pause on our journey. From time to time, we must stop on the path and look back. Not to long for what we have overcome, but to become aware of how far we have come, and how much we have accomplished.

The old man closed his eyes and took a deep breath.

There it is, he said softly. The oasis isn't just

a place along the way; it's also a promise fulfilled. It's the embodiment of our dreams coming true.

The boy ran to the spring, drank eagerly, and watched his reflection tremble in the water. He clasped his hands again and scooped up some more. He realized that much of it slipped through his fingers, and he couldn't do anything about it.

Why does the water move even when there's no wind?. Why does it slip away as if by magic?  he asked.

Because life never stops, the old man said. Even in the deepest silence, something still beats. This water has traveled farther than we have. Perhaps it was once a cloud, or part of a sea, or a tear. Or perhaps it simply moistened a flowering garden. Everything in life has its journey.

The boy listened attentively.

So, will this place also pass away? The old man nodded.

Everything passes, my son. But there are moments we must pause to contemplate, because they are what give us the strength to carry on. Just because something is going to happen doesn't mean we shouldn't enjoy it when it happens.

And why does it slip through our fingers even when we squeeze it tight? he asked.

Because life passes by, and if we don't pay attention, it slips away just as quickly and easily, the old man replied. Life is like a living being: it's born, it grows, it reproduces, and it dies. It has its cycle, even if we don't see it that way. The oasis isn't meant to be a permanent fixture, but rather a reminder that even in the middle of the desert, life is capable of flourishing.

Haven't you heard the story of the lotus flower, my son?

No, Grandfather. What's it about?

The lotus flower holds profound symbolism in various cultures, religions, and social circles. It's an aquatic plant that closely resembles the beautiful stones of this river. It grows in swampy places, in the mud, and yet its flower rises above the surface to bloom, elevated, fragrant, and elegant. It's a perfect symbol associated with purity, rebirth, strength, and overcoming adversity. A powerful metaphor for resilience and spiritual enlightenment.

The boy lowered his gaze.

And what if one stays here forever?

One withers, the old man replied serenely. The water of the oasis wasn't meant to stagnate, but to nourish the journey. Whoever lingers too long in their rest forgets the purpose of the path and of the journey.

It's not about altering its cycle, but about living it consciously and facing it with dignity, he added. To help you understand better, I'll give you the perfect example:

Imagine a man who exercises, eats well, gets enough rest, avoids excessive alcohol and tobacco, manages stress well, maintains a positive attitude, and has good social connections with family and friends. He's expected to live a long life. But this doesn't prevent him from one day experiencing gray hair, wrinkles, and high blood pressure. No matter how well we take care of ourselves, these things are inevitable. Some experience them sooner than others, but in the end, if we don't die young, we all experience them.

They fell silent. The sound of the river mingled with the murmur of the wind, as if all of nature were uttering a wordless prayer.

Master, the boy whispered, and where does the river end?

In the sea, the old man replied, where all waters meet. It is the destiny of all that lives: to return to its source, to unite with the eternal.

The boy smiled, finally understanding the mystery of flow.

So, when I hear the river, will I also hear my soul?

Exactly, the old man said. Because water speaks the language of life, and whoever learns to listen to it, learns to live. Because every human being is like a river seeking its sea, and on that journey, what matters is not arriving, but learning to flow with gratitude, with awareness, with dignity, without forgetting that every stone along the way is also part of the water's music.

The old man sat up and gazed at the horizon.

Come, my son. The journey continues. May the river teach you not to fear change, and may the oasis remind you that peace is also part of the journey. And as they walked away, the murmur of the water faded into the distance like an ancient song that kept flowing, and like a wordless meringue that reminded them that true wisdom lies not in arriving, but in learning to flow.

# CHAPTER XIV
# THE PATHS OF ALL

Dawn was breaking like a flower on the horizon. The old man and the child walked along a wide, quiet path, where the footprints of many travelers intertwined, without distinction of age, race, or origin, yet no one was to be seen. Each step raised a light golden dust, as if the ground itself wanted to remind them that all of us, absolutely all of us, without exception, are part of the same earth.

Filled with energy by the opportunity of a new day, they continued steadfastly on their journey. And as they walked a few more miles, they reached a section of the path where some of the owners of those footprints were gathered. Many travelers: men, women, the elderly, children.

Walkers of different faces, colors, and accents could be seen. People from different lands and ethnicities. Each carried their burden, their story, their destiny. All shared the same path.

The boy watched in silence, marveling at the diversity that unfolded before his eyes, and his mind was filled with questions:

Teacher, why do some paths separate people? he asked sadly. I've heard that in some places they don't let those who are different walk together.

Why do some walk apart? Why do some seem unable to accept others? The old man took a deep breath, gazing at the horizon.

Because many still haven't understood, he said serenely that the path doesn't belong to us. No one owns the path; we all walk it by the grace of life. It doesn't matter the color of your skin, your creed, or where you come from. On the path, we are all equal. We all laugh, we all suffer, we all dream. They still haven't understood that the path belongs to everyone. And the more we believe the ground is only ours, the further we stray from the truth. No one owns the earth we walk on, nor the air we breathe. We all come from the same dust, and in the end, to it we shall return. Color, belief, language, or flag are merely fleeting garments of the soul.

But aren't we all the same? The boy insisted.

When the sun rises, it shines on everyone. When the rain falls, it soaks everyone equally. That's how it should be, said the old man. On the true path, the color of your skin is but a shadow upon the light of your soul. The language you speak, the clothes you wear, and where you come from, the faith you profess, or the love you choose... none of that changes what you are: a traveler in search of meaning.

Continuing their journey, they walked for a while in silence until they reached a clearing where the wind blew strongly, carrying new, distant voices. Quickly and resolutely, they crossed that stretch, entering the very heart of the new crowd: voices arguing, pointing, trying to impose their truth.

The boy frowned.

Why do they want everyone to think the same? he asked.

Because fear, my son, said the old man, is the oldest of tyrants. There are those who fear losing their power if they let others think for themselves. There are groups, institutions, and even entire kingdoms that have tried to dictate what the human heart should feel. They use their flags, their temples, or their laws, but the end is the same: to control the course of others.

The boy lowered his gaze, confused.

So, what should we do?

We must be wise, said the old man calmly. Not everything that glitters is true, nor does every loud voice deserve to be heard. To walk freely does not mean to wander aimlessly, but to do so with awareness and respect. And above all, never stop loving.

Like water carried by a river, they continued their pilgrimage without stopping.

They walked in silence for a few more miles, while the murmur of the wind carried the voices of other travelers. Voices with a different tone and a different melody. They were laughs, varied accents, songs that this time spoke of hope. In the air, songs with different accents could be heard, laughter in different languages, but all harmonized in the same tone: that of shared life.

The old man stopped and pointed to the horizon.

Look, boy. All those faces, though different, carry the same sparkle in their eyes: the desire to arrive, to learn, to love. Deep down, there are no paths for one or the other; there is only one path that unites us all: the path of respect, dignity, and peace.

The boy pondered for a moment and said in a gentle voice:

So, when someone despises another, they also lose themselves.

Exactly, the old man agreed.  Those who do not respect forget their own origins. Those who do not recognize the dignity of others lose their own. Always remember, child: respect for the rights of others is peace. And peace is the most beautiful flower that grows in the soil of respect and love. To be just, to be dignified, and to live with compassion that is what makes the journey worthwhile. Only those who walk with love can truly go far, and only those who are just will one day be able to achieve happiness.

They continued on their way. At every step, new travelers joined them: women, men, young, old, all different, yet united by a common destiny. The sun, high above, seemed to bless this caravan of souls who, regardless of their past or their differences, had understood the greatest lesson of the journey: that inclusion is not an idea, but a way of loving. And that whoever loves, never walks alone.

Master, said the child, when we all walk together, I feel the path is easier.

The old man looked at him with a calm smile and replied: Because in unity there is strength, child. He who walks alone can advance, but he who walks with others goes further. And when we live not only for ourselves, but also for others, then we truly have a desire to live.

The sun was already high when they stopped to rest under a tree. The old man closed his eyes and murmured:

To truly live is to allow everyone to live as well. Inclusion is not an idea; it is a way of loving. And whoever loves, never walks alone.

# CHAPTER XV

# THE MARKET OF CONSCIOUSNESS

At night, the same moon shone with a million dreams to dream.

And in the morning, the same sun rose with a billion sunrises to discover.

With a handful of unknowns, the boy kept asking. A child with a brain pregnant with dreams began to give birth to a handful of crazy ideas. Every word, every doubt, and every gesture drew in his gaze an insatiable hunger to learn.

The old man was a light of coherence in the darkness of the chaos of innocence in a hostile world. He didn't miss a single opportunity to guide the child, sowing in his heart the seeds of reason and spirit.

While trying to explain something, the old man bit his tongue and, with a smile, said jokingly:

I don't think that's the best way to eat meat in this place.

The boy didn't laugh; perhaps he didn't understand, or perhaps he was too focused on his next question.

Soaking the beret he held in his hand with sweat from his brow, he asked:

What do you think is the compass for this journey, Master? Values, intelligence, family, resilience, or solidarity?

The old man looked at him serenely.

The worst thing a man can do, he said, is to renounce his principles and deceive himself because you are a witness to your own deception.

Always remember that a man is what he shows outwardly, plus the sum of his thoughts. He is not only himself, but the legacy of those who came before him and the reflection of those who will come after. My legacy is what I represent of my ancestors, and the footprints I leave for those who will one day walk after me.

And does not abandoning your principles and values make you a successful man? The boy interrupted.

The old man smiled tenderly.

Success, my son, is not about going the farthest, but about emerging with the greatest possible dignity from the depths of your being. Never be afraid to make mistakes, because mistakes teach more than triumphs. But be afraid of losing your conscience, because it is the only mirror that doesn't lie.

The old man spoke this way because he knew that human wickedness had become a kind of cancer that begins by eating a single cell, until it devours everything it touches.

Birds can distinguish between day and night, he continued, but modern man seems to have lost the ability to distinguish between good and evil. The noise of the world has robbed him of his inner hearing.

The boy remained thoughtful.

But, Grandfather, almost everyone we've seen on this path strives to reach the end successfully. Why do they do that?

Because they confuse success with purpose, the old man replied. If there's anything I wish you to pursue, it's not success, but peace. Because success, through effort, comes on its own.

As we walk this path, we piece together the puzzle of our own lives. Success comes only when the soul is calm.

When you live in peace, the noise of the outside world doesn't distract you.

They walked a long way until they reached a large rest stop. Flowers filled its courtyards, and it had multiple entrances. Several entrances, but none with physical doors. Its architecture combined Oriental, Baroque, and Victorian styles, as if it were a testament to many intertwined cultures. It was a testament to the originality and blend of its founders.

The place was majestic, and its clientele diverse. There were all kinds of faces, languages, and customs. The atmosphere was vibrant, and every corner seemed to breathe the mix of humanity.

There was no common ground, but everyone had come seeking physical and mental rest. Some brought valuable belongings, defended even with their lives; others, nothing more than the clothes on their backs. No one lived there, no one managed it. It was like a train station: people got on and off, but the train kept moving.

It was a space for awareness, a test of character. There, comfort and material possessions were not priorities. It was about overcoming the ego, about shining the light of understanding upon ignorance.

The old man observed attentively and said:

This, my son, is the "Market of Conscience".

The boy looked at him, curious.

And what is sold here, Master?

The old man replied: Here, no one sells gold or buys silver.

Here, we trade in the invisible: morality, truth, respect, and dignity. Here, we buy friendship, service, and rest without coins.

This place seeks to change the traditional paradigm that needs are satisfied with money, its equivalent, or bureaucracy.

Here, it is understood that where there is nothing, everything is safe; but where there is money, there are no friends, no honor, no culture, no patriotism, no science… only self-interest.

The boy frowned.

So how do you buy?

With conscience, the old man replied.

In a world where everything has its price and value, where you are generally worth what you own, the path leads you to buy, and to buy without money.

Where there is money, there is the possibility of corruption. But when you buy with awareness, you do so without deception. What is priceless is a gift, and what is a gift has no limits. On the path, there are no borders; limits are created by people.

They walked to the center of the inn, where a large sign was engraved on stone with indelible ink. In majestic letters, it read:

"To those who are thirsty, come and buy without money."

The boy read it aloud and asked:

Why does it say to those who are thirsty?

Because the thirsty are the ones who seek, the old man replied.

He who is full of himself has no room to learn. He who is not thirsty for justice, for love, or for truth, dies of empty abundance.

The old man stroked his beard and continued:

Wherever there is a transaction involving money, there is a risk of corruption, manipulation, and lies. On the other hand, when what is bought is with conscience, the price is paid with integrity, and the soul emerges victorious. Here, the transaction is of the soul.

Later, they both stopped before a stream.

The water ran clear and bright, and its sound mingled with the birdsong.

They followed its course until it led them to an oasis hidden among trees. The water flowed like life in the middle of the desert.

It was a marvelous pool of natural water, flowing like manna falling from the sky in the midst of a rampant famine, or like the air a mummy receives upon emerging from its sarcophagus after a thousand years of sleep, having recharged its batteries for ten thousand more.

There was no beach or sand, only the great willows, with their thick trunks, extravagant branches of ornate foliage, and lanceolate, whitish leaves that swayed gently in the breeze, seeming to murmur prayers to the wind.

They gazed at each other in wonder, understanding that this place was more than a rest: it was a lesson.

There they sat down to rest.

The old man cupped some water in his hands and let it run through his fingers.

You see, son? That's what conscience is like.

It's hard to keep it clean, but when you manage it, it reflects the truth.

The boy remained silent, contemplating the moon's reflection in the water.

So, master… who watches over this market?

No one, the old man replied.

And that's precisely why it's a test.

Here, where no one is watching, is where you truly show who you are. A person's true worth is measured when there are no witnesses.

The old man gazed at the horizon and concluded:

The marketplace of consciousness has no owner or guardian, because you are the guardian yourself. The path merely offers you the place, but you decide what you buy and what you sell.

And remember: what is bought without money has an invisible price... but with eternal value.

The boy nodded slowly, understanding that this resting place was not just a respite on the journey, but a mirror of the soul. In a serene voice, he said:

Grandfather, I think I'm beginning to understand... The true marketplace is the soul. And the old man, smiling, replied:

That's right, my son. In the marketplace of consciousness, only those who are thirsty buy… and only those who have light receive.

As the sun set behind the willows, the old man stood up and added in a firm voice:

Son, one day you will return to this place.

And when that happens, don't come to buy… come to offer what you have learned.

The boy smiled, and together they continued walking under the golden glow of the sunset, knowing that they had just left the only market where the valid currency was conscience.

# CHAPTER XVI

# THE ECHOES OF MEMORY

The path stretched out beneath a gentle breeze, and the old man walked slowly, observing the trees that seemed to whisper stories carried on the wind from time immemorial. The curious boy gazed at everything in wonder, as if every stone had a story to tell.

Master, the boy asked, why do trees remember so much? The old man smiled. Because their roots hold what they have lived through.

The boy walked for a few minutes in silence, lost in thought, watching as the old man began to caress a stone he had picked up from the ground.

Why a stone? The boy wondered, wordlessly.

It seemed a simple gesture, but there was a deep tenderness in his gaze, as if that stone held a secret for the old man.

Why do you keep that stone, Master? the boy asked, unable to stop himself.

The old man smiled without answering immediately. Then, raising his eyes to the horizon, he said in a serene voice:

Because on the journey, my son, memory is the most precious stone we carry. Memory, my child, is the soul of time. It holds the traces of who we were, the voices of those who loved us, the lessons of our falls, and the music of our victories. Memory can be a balm… or a wound. It can be a lamp that guides us forward or a chain that binds us to yesterday.

The boy listened in silence, as if each word hung suspended in the air.

So… Can memory set us free or imprison us? he asked.

That's right, the old man replied. It can be the bridge that connects you to hope or the chain that binds you to the past. It can be the reason we reconcile and feel affection, or the reason we resist moving forward. Memory can depress us, or it can propel us to be better.

The boy remained thoughtful. So, can memory help us or harm us?

That's true, the old man replied.

It allows us to create new things, because memories teach us how to live better, how to avoid mistakes, and how to repeat what has served us well.

But it can also be a prison if we cling too tightly to what can no longer return.

For a brief moment, the boy walked in silence, glancing back now and then, as if searching for something he had left behind on the path.

The old man, noticing his attitude, smiled serenely again and said:

Memory, my child, is the invisible bridge between what we were, what we are, and what we can become. It holds the fragrance of happy days, but also the echo of our tears. It is a powerful ally… although sometimes it can also become a shadow.

The boy looked up curiously.

And why a shadow, Master?

Because if we only live looking back, the old man replied, we risk stumbling over what is in front of us. Memory should help us move forward, not stagnate.

The boy nodded slowly.

So… memory can also help us to love and forgive?

That's right, the old man said tenderly. Memory is the workshop of the soul. It holds the faces of those we love, the words of those who hurt us, and the lessons we learned along the way. It teaches us to forgive, because it reminds us of what we are capable of losing if we don't. It teaches us to love, because it takes us back to the moments when our hearts beat with gratitude.

The old man continued, in a more reflective tone:

Memory teaches us to forgive, because it reminds us how much we ourselves have failed. It teaches us to love, because it revives the gestures and words that marked our lives. And it also teaches us to weep, because it brings back the echo of those who are gone.

Every tear has its origin in memory. That is why memory is human, and without it, the heart would be like a guitar without strings.

Then the old man paused for a moment, gathered a handful of earth, and let the wind crumble it between his fingers.

His voice deepened, almost solemn:

Memory, my son, is to our lives what oxygen is to breathing. Without it, the soul suffocates.

Memory is to our brain what faith is to our spirit: a vital impulse that gives meaning to who we are.

Without memory, there is no reasoning, no continuity, no identity.

It is the fuel that feeds our thoughts and the flame of conscience. The beacon that illuminates our decisions, the voice that reminds us who we are and where we are going.

Thanks to memory, we remember our obligations and duties to our loved ones, to our neighbors, and to ourselves.

It is memory that calls us to commitment, that prevents us from forgetting where we come from and who helped us get here.

The boy listened attentively, as if each word fell into his heart like a seed.

And what should we do with sad memories? he asked timidly.

The old man took a deep breath.

Be grateful for them.

Because they made us wiser.

Sadness also teaches, even if its method is harsh.

The memory of pain reminds us that we are capable of enduring, of getting up, of continuing to walk when we thought we couldn't go on.

The old man stopped, and looking at the boy tenderly, said:

But don't forget this: we must also create new memories.

Don't live only in yesterday. Live the present intensely, because what you do today will be the memory that embraces you tomorrow.

Walk, laugh, help, love… every moment counts.

The day memory fades, only what you planted in the hearts of others will remain.

The boy gazed at the horizon and smiled:

So, teacher, every step we take… is it a memory we are building?

Exactly, little one, replied the old man. Memory is the echo of the soul, and the soul, when it loves, never forgets.

Strive, then, to ensure that your footprints are not erased by time, but rather blossom in the memories of others.

Only in this way, when the body tires and the voice is silenced, will you continue to live on in the paths of those with whom you once walked.

After a brief silence, the old man continued:

There are different kinds of memory, and each one fulfills its purpose on the path of life.

There is social memory, which belongs to the

people. It is the collective conscience of what a nation has lived through. When people forget the pain of injustice or the lies of their rulers, they stumble over the same stones again. When a society forgets the grievances it has endured, it becomes easy to deceive. Corrupt rulers know this: they offer crumbs, brief periods of apparent well-being, and the people forget the pain of entire years. It is sad to see societies that, for a moment of comfort or fleeting promises, forget years of abuse and deception. Whoever loses their social memory also loses their dignity. To remember is not to hold a grudge; it is to learn not to repeat the past.

And spiritual memory? the child asked.

That is the anchor of the soul, the old man replied. It is what keeps us firm when the winds of fashion and fleeting beliefs try to sway us. It is what keeps our faith strong, whatever it may be. We must not let ourselves be swept away by fleeting beliefs or trends that promise instant answers. True spirituality demands consistency and effort. This isn't about fanaticism, but about remaining steadfast in what is fundamental, even if it hurts, even if it's difficult. Faith cultivated through hardship becomes certainty.

Some change their faith as easily as they change their clothes, seeking what is easy, what is new, what requires the least effort. But true spiritual memory consists of remaining rooted in what is fruitful, in what bears fruit, even if it demands sacrifice. This isn't about fanaticism, but about consistency, about fidelity to what is true. Spiritual memory teaches us to remember where we come from and to whom we belong, so that we don't get lost in the noise of the world.

And personal memory? The boy persisted, with a curious smile.

Ah, personal memory… the old man said, gazing at the horizon. That is the most intimate of all. It is the memory that holds the moments that shaped us. It is what transports us to happy days and invites us to remain in them. It is what holds the moments that made us feel alive: a sunrise, a hug, a melody, a voice. But it can also become a trap if we refuse to move forward, if we want to live forever in those memories.

We must be careful: clinging to the past prevents us from living in the present. We must remember without becoming prisoners of memory. It is beautiful to look back, but we must remember that the journey continues. Memory should not be a prison, but a garden where the flowers of yesterday perfume today. Good memories are nourishment, not a dwelling.

The boy, frowning, asked:

And why are there those who prefer that others not remember?

Because a person without memory is like a wanderer without a destination, the old man replied. Ignorance is the most powerful weapon of those who seek to dominate. When we don't remember, we stop questioning. That's why, my son, there are those who extinguish the lamp of memory... to keep us in the dark.

Then he paused and added gravely:

True poverty lies not in the lack of material wealth, but in the absence of freedom. And the only true wealth is precisely freedom, the kind that allows us to reach our full potential. It's like a lamp lit in a dark room: it's not about decorating the room, but about illuminating it. Why don't some want it to be lit? Because they prefer us to be blind... that way we're easier to control."

The old man stopped, looked at the horizon, and continued in a measured voice:

The societies that endure are not the most scientifically advanced, nor the most militarily powerful. They are those that are sustained by ethical values. Knowledge can create tools, but only values know how to use them well. Without ethics, knowledge becomes a weapon. Without principles, science can destroy what it once promised to protect. That is why moral memory and the value of dignity are essential for the survival of any civilization.

The boy looked at him curiously.

And what does that have to do with war, teacher? The old man lowered his gaze.

Everything, my son. Thousands of years ago, the Greeks and the Trojans clashed over power, pride, and ambition. History remembers it as the "Trojan War", but it was really a war of human ego. Throughout history, many empires have fallen into the same trap. The wise call it "Thucydides' Trap": when an emerging power threatens an established one, and fear, more than reason, ignites conflict.

The boy remained thoughtful.

So... memory can also teach us how to avoid war.

Exactly. When we remember the mistakes of the past, we sow the seeds of peace for the future.

The old man paused for a moment, picked up a leaf from the ground, and examined it closely.

The wise traveler not only remembers, he said finally, but also cultivates and exercises his memory. He learns from the past without becoming enslaved by it, retains what is essential, and lets go of what weighs him down. Memory is the witness of the soul; it reminds us of our obligations to others, to ourselves, and to life.

And as he continued on his way, the old man concluded in a soft but firm voice:

Cultivate your memory, child, but do so wisely. Remember enough not to get lost… but forget what is necessary to keep walking.

# CHAPTER XVII

# THE PATH OF FREEDOM

As the birds awoke, dawn broke over the mountains, and the sun's rays caressed the path where the old man and the boy walked in silence. The wind blew softly along the path, stirring the dry leaves that fell at their feet, bringing with it a profound calm, as if the universe were listening.

Suddenly, the old man spoke in a calm and firm voice:

You know, child? Freedom is the foundation of all democracy. Without it, the path grows dark, loses its light, and humankind loses its dignity.

All people are born equal… not because their bodies are the same, nor their faces the same, but because they all have the same right to walk, to decide, and to dream.

That is the true meaning of equality: not a copy, but an opportunity. The curious boy asked: And what does it mean to be free, teacher? To do whatever one wants? The old man smiled slightly.

No, my child. To be free is not to do whatever one wants, but to do what is right without fear.

Freedom is not measured by the absence of rules, but by the presence of conscience. It is born in the soul, not in decrees.

Freedom is the very essence of life.

God, or nature, depending on how each person understands it, placed us in the world to walk the path with awareness, with responsibility, with respect. And in that sense, all people are born equal... Equal not because they have the same strength, the same tastes, or the same talents, but because they have the same right to decide their own course.

And remember something important: what is forbidden becomes desirable.

That is why those who are truly free are not tempted by what is forbidden, but choose what is right even when no one is watching.

And why are there those who want to take that right away from others? the child asked.

The old man sighed.

Because many confuse power with guidance.

When people lose their passion for freedom, they entrust their path to those who promise to lead them, but who in reality bind them.

And that happens when faith, hope, and trust are placed in a man and not in the principles, values, and ideas that should guide the way.

The weak place their faith in leaders; the strong, in their convictions. The former live in fear, the latter with dignity.

So... said the boy, shouldn't we follow anyone?

Yes, replied the old man, we should follow those who remind us that we, too, can think, decide, and act with conscience.

The true leader is not the one who commands, but the one who teaches others to be free. Because freedom is not imposed, it is inspired.

They walked a few more steps as the sun began to rise behind the mountains. The old man continued:

Freedom is not a flag that is waved only in times of struggle; it is a flame that must be protected every day.

It is the ability to choose without harming, to think without fear, to live without chains. And on this path of life, my son, we all have the same right to walk, although not everyone chooses to do so with the same courage, and at the same pace.

The boy lowered his gaze, thoughtful, while the old man continued:

Freedom, my son, is not a gift bestowed upon us, but a responsibility we must cherish.

Many expect the government or their neighbors to provide them with all the crutches they need to survive, but those crutches, in time, paralyze them in their souls.

They make them dependent, incapable of walking on their own.

Freedom requires effort, courage, and, above all, the will to stand on one's own two feet.

The man who does not fight for his livelihood, nor for his ideals, ends up accepting any yoke rather than fall.

The boy looked up, intrigued:

And happiness, teacher? Is it also a right? The old man nodded gently.

Happiness isn't guaranteed, my child. No one can promise you happiness. The only thing that should be guaranteed is the opportunity to seek it.

Each person must forge their own path, make mistakes, get up, and keep going.

To expect someone else to walk for you, or to carry you the entire journey, is to renounce your freedom and your very essence. Because whoever depends on another to live soon depends on another to think as well.

The wind blew strongly, raising the dust from the path. The old man gazed at the horizon and continued: People who lose their passion for freedom end up being led by leaders who promise security in exchange for obedience.

And that, my son, is the beginning of all

servitude.

The weak place their faith in men; the strong, in principles, values, and ideas. Only those who walk guided by their conscience can truly say they are free.

The child watched him attentively. Then the old man stopped, took a deep breath, and in a firmer voice, almost as if he were preaching, added:

My son, many confuse poverty with a lack of wealth, but I tell you a great truth: the only true wealth is freedom.

Freedom allows us to become the best version of ourselves. It's a lamp in the middle of a dark room.

It's not about decorating the room, but about illuminating it. And do you know why some don't want the room lit?

Because they prefer us to be blind, so we're more easily controlled.

A people without light, without thought, and without freedom, is a people on their knees.
That's why, my son, never let them extinguish your inner lamp, because whoever loses the light

ends up loving their own darkness. And ends up living in the midst of a crisis of their way of life.

The boy, his eyes wide with wonder, said:

So, teacher, freedom is like air...

Exactly, replied the old man.

The air isn't seen, but it's felt. And when it's lacking, there's no life. That's what freedom is like: invisible, but vital.

Take care of it as you take care of your breath, as if it were the apple of your eye. Defend it with the truth, protect it with your dignity, and never surrender it to anyone who would think or decide for you.

They both continued on their way, and the old man concluded, his voice seeming to melt into the wind:

Remember this, my child: He who walks in freedom walks in the light. And he who walks in the light will never be a slave to darkness.

# CHAPTER XVIII

# THE CROSSROADS OF DISCORD

The old man and the boy were walking along the path when they came to a large crossroads.

Three paths lay before them: one wide and bright, filled with laughter and voices; another narrow and steep, covered with stones; and a third, more discreet, shrouded in a serene twilight.

This way, said the boy, pointing to the wide path.  Look how beautiful and clear it is. The sun shines unobstructed, and the wind blows in our favor. People are laughing in the distance; they seem happy. Surely this is the right one.

The old man, leaning on his staff, watched in silence.

Sometimes the brightest light blinds the eyes. Light doesn't always mean clarity, my son, he replied calmly.  I prefer the narrow path. It teaches more, even if it hurts. Sometimes, what shines brightest is what deceives most.

The boy frowned.

And why does the difficult path always have to be the best?

I don't want to suffer to learn. I want to live with joy. You always want to do everything slowly, as if time didn't matter. I want to live now!

It's not always the difficulty that teaches, said the old man with a gentle smile, but the easy almost never transforms. You always run without thinking about what you leave behind. Life isn't just about speed.

The disagreement grew, and for the first time on their long journey, they turned their backs on each other and decided to separate.

The boy took the wide path, confident. The old man chose the steep path, determined. The day wore on, and each soon discovered his own mistake: The boy found soulless noise. He soon found himself among empty voices, false laughter, and a horizon that led nowhere. The old man, on the other hand, found a path so hard that his strength failed him before he reached the first bend, and the frustration caused him a pain that completely overwhelmed him. He found only lessons without solace.

Something inside them broke: they couldn't walk apart.

Hours passed. Both, exhausted, dissatisfied, and confused, returned to their starting point. There, under the shade of the same tree where they had argued before, they met again, as if nothing had happened.

You were right, said the boy, his gaze downcast. The wide path had no soul, only noise.

And so did you, replied the old man. The narrow one taught me, yes… but it taught me that not all lessons require suffering. Perhaps we were both wrong.

Upon meeting, they understood that their disagreement had not been so different from the one echoing in the distance.

In the distance, raised voices and arguments could be heard, and a tense atmosphere hung in the air. Men and women were arguing, some pointing one way, others the other. Each defended their position as if truth itself depended on it. Yielding was not an option.

From where they stood, they could hear a

crowd arguing in the valley below.

People shouting about who was right, who possessed the truth, who should lead the others. The noise was deafening, as if the whole world were tearing itself apart from within.

Look, said the boy, they're arguing too.

Yes, replied the old man, the world is full of paths and voices that believe themselves to be unique. And each one defends their light without realizing that they also cast their shadow.

The boy stopped and looked around in amazement.

Master, why are they fighting?  he asked. Isn't it the same path we all travel? The old man rested his staff on the ground and observed in silence.

Yes, my son… but many believe that only their path is the correct one. They confuse truth with custom, reason with pride. Look closely: all those paths lead to the same mountain, but each one wants the others to follow theirs.

The boy frowned.

So, which path should we take?

The old man smiled calmly.

The one who allows you to walk in peace, without hurting anyone. Discord is born when the mind tries to impose what the heart doesn't understand. He who always seeks to be right ends up losing his serenity.

The boy thought about it for a moment.

But teacher, what if they are wrong? The old man replied: Truth doesn't need to be defended with shouts. It only needs to be lived. The righteous person doesn't impose their path; they walk it with humility, and their example convinces more than a thousand words.

As they walked on, the crowd continued arguing. Some watched them; others continued their disputes.

The boy stopped once more, looking back, and said:

They seem so busy being right that they've forgotten to keep walking. The old man nodded. That's what happens to many, my son. They get stuck at the crossroads of discord, trapped in the noise of pride, without realizing that the path continues only for those who choose peace.

It was then that they looked toward the third path, the one neither of them had considered: the dark path, which seemed unappealing, but had a serene murmur, as if the wind wanted to guide them, and as if its murmur seemed to speak to them.

What is most visible is not always the truest, said the old man.

Nor is what is darkest, most fearsome, added the child.

Perhaps the truth doesn't shout, whispered the old man.

Perhaps it is only heard when you walk together, replied the child.

They took the path without further discussion. They held hands again and walked forward together, without certainty, but with their trust restored.

As they walked, they noticed that the gloom was transforming into a soft light, the kind that doesn't blind but illuminates. And that the darkness was transforming into serene clarity, and they understood that the right path was neither the wide nor the narrow, but the one they could walk together. They also understood that the right path isn't always chosen by reason or emotion, but by the humility to agree and give space to others.

They walked a few more steps, and the old man, moving forward with hope, added in a serene voice:

Remember this: not all disagreement is an enemy of truth, but all truth loses its light and credibility when it is used to divide. Always walk with a clear conscience, and let silence speak where voices are confused. The boy smiled, understanding that the true traveler doesn't need to win arguments to move forward, only to keep a pure heart.

Then the old man placed his hand on the boy's shoulder and said:

In unity there is strength. When two hearts walk in the same direction, fear becomes light, and the path becomes home. On the path, as in life, it's not about who is right, but about learning not to lose sight of each other.

The boy, looking toward the horizon, replied:

So, master, I learned that it's not about being right, but about mutual support.

They walked in silence, while the crowd behind them faded into its own noise. Before them, the path unfolded like a promise, simple and true, where peace was not the destination, but the way of walking. And so, as the sun broke through the mist, they continued on their way, leaving behind the murmur of discord and entering once more into the stillness of the road.

# CHAPTER XIX

# THE UNSUNG HEROES AND THE CYRENIAN

A round of applause for the unsung heroes!

Every significant event in life a victory, a healing, an achievement is made possible by those who, unseen, make it happen.

We know the names of those at the forefront: the leaders, the heroes, the brave ones who face the battle. But we rarely acknowledge those who, from the shadows, blow the wind that propels their wings.

Wars are won by those who wield weapons, yes… but behind every warrior are hands that sewed the uniform, forged the steel of the weapon, and prepared the food for their sustenance.

In hospitals, surgeons save lives with admirable precision; however, their success also depends on the anonymous individuals who clean, sterilize, and prepare each instrument.

The world is sustained by them: by the silent ones, those who don't seek applause, but without whom nothing could go on.

They are the unsung heroes of existence, the invisible foundations of goodness.

The old man and the boy reached a crossroads where a wall stood covered in names written in charcoal. Some still glowed dark; others, almost erased by time.

What is this wall? The boy asked.

It is the memory of those who helped other travelers, the old man replied. Each name was someone who lent a hand, a word, or a kind gesture… and went on their way without expecting anything in return.

The boy ran his finger over an almost invisible name.

And why are they forgotten?

Because life goes on, the old man said sadly. The memory of the heart sometimes grows dormant. We don't always remember those who lent us a hand at the right moment.

They fell silent. Then the old man continued:

An unsung hero can be a neighbor who shared their bread, a teacher who showed you the way, a friend who listened when you needed it most, a boss who believed in you, or even a stranger who lifted you up when you fell. Even if their names fade, their actions remain etched in our souls.

The boy thought for a few seconds and asked:

So, how can we thank them if they're no longer here, or if we don't even know who they were?

With gratitude, the old man replied. Gratitude doesn't require physical presence. Giving thanks in your heart is honoring all those who supported us without asking for anything in return. When you give thanks from the soul, you honor all those who helped you, even if you can't thank them in person.

The old man gazed at the horizon and added serenely:

Those who are grateful never walk alone, because they carry in their memory the strength of all the unsung heroes who supported them.

So today I want to give thanks for all of them,

the boy said, touching his chest.

Do it, son, said the old man. And never forget that one day you, too, will be an unsung hero in someone's life.

The sun was beginning to set, and the afternoon was covered in a soft gray, when the old man and the boy reached a steep stretch of the path. Weariness was felt with every step, the air seemed denser, heavier, and the path seemed longer than ever.

The old man and the boy walked in silence, as if the wind had carried away their words. Dust mingled with their weariness, and each step was a battle against discouragement.

The old man, with his trembling staff, moved forward with difficulty. The boy watched him, worried, not knowing how to ease his burden.

Master, said the boy in a subdued voice, why does the path become so difficult sometimes? There are times when one feels one can go no further. That one's feet are heavy, that dreams ache, and that one's heart turns to stone.

The old man took a deep breath and smiled

weakly. Because that's life, son. There are paths where our strength fails, and yet, we must continue. It's the weight of the invisible cross we all bear. No one walks without it. But listen to this: when the soul is exhausted, life, in its mysterious compassion, always sends us a Simon of Cyrene… someone to help us go on when we think we can't go on anymore.

The boy looked up, intrigued.

A Cyrenian? What's that?

Yes, the old man replied. He smiled, and his eyes lit up with the tenderness of someone remembering something sacred.

The Cyrenian was that man who helped carry a cross that wasn't his own. Another's cross, without seeking it, without wanting it, but moved by something greater than himself. And in life, we also find those who help us carry our own. When we need them most, when our strength fails, and the horizon darkens. They don't always stay long; sometimes they only appear for an instant, but that instant is enough to renew the soul.

The boy remained silent, meditating, while the breeze gently stirred the trees.

Master... did you also have a Cyrenian?

The old man looked at the horizon and smiled, as if he saw a face that time had erased.

Yes, my son. When I was young, I too wandered through strange lands and thought I had lost everything. I carried within me a hurricane of dreams and fears.

I encountered disappointments, closed doors, and voices that refused to listen. And when I was about to give up, someone looked at me with compassion and said:

"Keep going, there's still a long way to go."

The boy looked up, a spark of hope in his eyes.

And what happened next?

I kept going, the old man replied. Because that's what true and timely help does: it doesn't take the burden away, but it reminds you that you can still move forward.

The boy, his face burning with understanding, asked fearfully:

And what if one day I get tired and no one shows up?

The old man bent down and placed a hand on the boy's shoulder.

Then, my son, remember that we are all called to be like Simon of Cyrene on someone's path. If you can't find anyone to help you, be the one to help. Because when you lift another up, the weight of your own cross becomes lighter.

The sun was beginning to peek through the clouds, and the path was regaining its color. The old man took a deep breath, closed his eyes, and said softly: Never forget this, little traveler: the Cyrenians don't announce their arrival, but they are always there. They appear when life becomes an uphill climb, when the soul grows weary, and the horizon darkens. They are proof that goodness walks disguised as a friend, and that no heart is redeemed alone.

As they spoke, a young traveler approached from a distance. He wore a serene smile and carried a water skin. Seeing them weary, he stopped.

Do you need help?  he asked kindly.

The old man looked at him gratefully.

The path is long, and the shade is scarce. If you would like to walk a stretch with us, we would be grateful.

The young man nodded.

No one should walk alone when the day weighs heavily on their shoulders, he said, offering the water skin to the old man.

They drank together, and the air seemed to grow lighter, and their weariness seemed to vanish. For a while, they shared stories, laughter, and silences. The old man watched the young man with tenderness, recognizing in him the same strength he once possessed, the same hope that still shone in the boy's eyes.

When the sun hid behind the mountains, the young man stopped. I must go another way, he said, but thank you for letting me accompany you. The old man took his arm and replied: You don't know it, but today you were our Simon of Cyrene. Life always rewards those who help without expecting anything in return.
The young man smiled and continued on his way.

The old man and the boy continued on theirs in silence. After a while, the boy spoke: Master, do you think we will see him again?

The old man looked at the horizon.

Perhaps not, my son. But there are those who never say goodbye. They remain within us, in the way we learn to see and in the way we learn to help.

The boy reflected, understanding that true encounters along the way aren't measured in distance, but in the soul they leave their mark on.

As they resumed their walk, the old man added in a gentle voice:

Remember this, my son: even if circumstances harden your skin, don't let them harden your heart. Because a tender heart is the only one capable of recognizing the Cyrenians that life places in our path.

The anonymous heroes and the Cyrenians of the road are the invisible pillars of the world. They support without demanding, they love without being seen, and they lift us up when our souls stumble.

The boy nodded, and as they resumed their

walk, a gentle breeze seemed to caress their faces. It was as if the road itself were smiling at them, grateful to see them continue.

# CHAPTER XX

# UNDER THE TREE OF TIME

The path wound between gentle hills, and the wind carried the scent of damp earth and budding leaves.

The boy walked in silence, while the old man walked beside him, slower than usual, but with a burning gaze.

In the distance, on a small rise, stood a solitary tree.

Its branches, outstretched like the arms of a sage, offered shade and shelter to all who sought rest.

The old man pointed to the tree.

There, he said, the path holds one of its oldest lessons. When they arrived, the boy sat down beneath the leafy canopy.

The old man stood for a moment, gazing at the horizon before speaking:

This tree has seen many seasons pass. It has felt the weight of the rain, the embrace of the sun, and the lash of the wind. But it has never ceased to offer shade.

Do you know why?

The boy shook his head.

Because he learned that life doesn't always depend on what one receives, but on what one gives, said the old man, his voice mingling with the whisper of the wind. Gratitude, my son, is the root that sustains the soul in times of drought. It is the greatest feeling of appreciation and thankfulness, not only for what one has, but also for who one is.

The boy stroked the earth and said:

Then this tree must have very deep roots.

As deep as hope, replied the old man. Those who are grateful don't sink; they grow stronger. Even when the sky seems closed, the grateful person sees a crack through which the light enters.

They both remained silent.

The sun, filtering through the branches, cast

golden glimmers that seemed to slumber on the grass.

The old man continued:

But there is something else that strengthens the roots: forgiveness. Without it, the soul withers from within, even if the leaves still appear green.

The boy frowned.

And how does one learn to forgive? The old man sighed.

Forgiveness isn't forgetting, nor is it justifying. It's letting go of what cannot be changed. It's opening your hands so that pain ceases to possess you.

He was silent for a few seconds and added:

Sometimes we think we forgive others, but in truth, we free ourselves.

The wind blew strongly, and some leaves detached themselves from the tree, swirling in the air like small souls set free.

The boy watched them fall and said:

Perhaps the tree also forgives itself when it lets its leaves fall. The old man smiled.

Exactly. The wisdom of time lies in understanding that everything that falls does so to make room for something new. If a seed of wheat doesn't fall to the ground and die, it remains alone; but if it does, it bears much fruit.

They sat together under the trunk. The old man leaned back and closed his eyes.

Time doesn't just age, he murmured. It also teaches. He is a silent teacher who molds us without words.

The boy listened attentively.

And how do we know we've learned enough?

When we stop looking back in anger, the old man replied, and begin to look ahead with love.

The silence stretched out, serene.

In the distance, the sun slowly descended, painting the sky in shades of amber and violet. The old man picked up a fallen twig and traced a circle in the earth.

Everything you give comes back, my son. Sometimes in the form of a smile, sometimes in peace, sometimes in understanding.

He looked up and added:

Love is the sap that binds everything together. Without love, forgiveness withers, gratitude is forgotten, and wisdom becomes pride. It is the chlorophyll that gives the tree of life its green color.

The boy looked at him tenderly.

So love sustains the tree...

And sustains the traveler, the old man said softly. Love is the only thing that transcends time, the only thing that can cross the invisible bridges between life and eternity.

The wind calmed.

The tree stood firm, majestic, as if listening to the conversation. The old man placed his hand on the trunk and murmured: This tree is you, child. You are all its branches, all its falls, and all its blossoms.

Every wound will be a scar that gives you strength, every tear a root that anchors you deeper.

The child closed his eyes and rested his head against the trunk. He felt a faint pulse, as if the tree were breathing.

And in that instant, he understood that life also has a voice when it is silent. The old man rose slowly and said: Come. There is still a path to walk, but now you know how to stay on your feet. They both set off.

The tree remained behind, but its shadow followed them, invisible, accompanying their steps like a luminous memory.

# CHAPTER XXI

# THE DAY THE OLD MAN TRIPPED

The sun was barely peeking over the crags, casting a pale light on the cobblestone path, which was covered in dew at dawn. The boy walked lightly, as if his steps were wings. The old man walked with shorter strides than usual, leaning on his cane, which seemed to support not only his body, but also the weight of the years and the memories he carried.

He stopped suddenly in the middle of the path. His feet dragged dust, his breathing was heavy, and his hands trembled as he rested on his staff. The boy watched him intently, not daring to ask. There was something different in the air: a mixture of weariness and resignation, but also a strange calm, like the one that precedes a farewell.

Suddenly, the old man tripped over a piece of firewood hidden in the grass. The boy, who was playing with a branch, saw him fall to his knees and ran to help him, frightened.

Grandfather! Are you alright? he called out in a trembling voice.

The old man didn't answer immediately. He was breathing heavily, as if the air no longer came so easily to him. Then, he smiled weakly as he slowly sat up, his eyes reflecting the acceptance of the winters. His walking stick, once a symbol of wisdom, was now a real necessity.

Yes, son… I just stumbled, he said between pauses. But in life, stumbles aren't always signs of weakness. Sometimes, they're reminders that we're still walking.

After a few moments, the old man again showed signs of weakness, and the boy, sitting beside him, asked:

Master, are you hurt? Are you tired? Why are you walking so slowly today?

It's my body, little one… he said firmly. It's begun to tire of living. My body doesn't respond to me like it used to. I used to climb mountains as if they were hills; now, even a leaf makes me stumble. The body, my son, is like a tree in autumn: the branches still stand, but the leaves fall one by one. And when the trunk grows old, even the gentlest breeze makes it creak.

They sat in the shade of a palm tree. The old man stroked the rough bark of the tree and continued: Just as the body falls ill and tires, so too can the mind wither. There are those who have strong legs, but broken thoughts… And there are those who, though fragile of bone, hold up the world with the strength of their mind.

The boy, his eyes wide, asked:

So I must care for my mind as I care for my hands or my feet? The old man nodded, his voice almost a whisper: Yes. Because the body is earth and will return to the earth… but the mind is a river: if you poison it, your entire journey will turn bitter; if you keep it clear, all who walk beside you, and those who wait further ahead, will drink from you.

A profound silence enveloped the forest. The boy moved, stood up, and took the old man's staff to help him continue. He tried to understand that there is no greater wisdom than tending the inner river, because when the body falters, only the mind can continue to illuminate the path.

As they continued, the boy remained silent, not fully understanding. And the old man continued:

For some time now, I've felt my body giving

me warnings. Sometimes my chest coughs, and when the body coughs, the soul trembles… not out of fear, but because it knows that change is coming. The path doesn't belong to us; we only travel it. And there comes a point when the body asks for rest, but the spirit wants to continue.

The boy looked at him in amazement, and then, noticing his fatigue again, helped him sit down once more under a tree and asked:

Does that happen? Even if you want to keep walking? There, in the silence of the forest, the old man spoke calmly.

Yes. Even if the heart still has stories to tell, the body sometimes decides to rest first. The body is like a river… one day it flows strongly, another day it slows down. It's not just age: it's also how we take care of it. But listen carefully: as I already told you, the same thing happens with the mind.

The boy looked at him. Now more curious than ever, he asked:

Can the mind get sick, too?

Of course, replied the old man. If we fill it with anger, fear, or sadness, it becomes weak, like a tree rotting from the inside. If, on the other hand, we nourish it with gratitude, hope, and patience, it remains strong, even if the body begins to fail.

The boy treasured those words. And as he helped the old man to his feet again, he understood that health wasn't just about walking without tiring, but also about thinking and feeling clearly.

That day, the boy learned that one day, even his body would fail, but if he took care of his mind, his spirit would keep walking beyond any limit.

For days, the old man no longer led the way. It was the boy who gathered firewood, who prepared the food, who told stories at night to make him smile.

One night, while the old man dozed, the boy spoke softly to the fire:

And what if the mind gets sick too? What if one day I forget who I am, or why I'm walking?

The old man opened one eye and said in a hoarse voice:

That's why, little one, you have to tend your mind like you tend a garden, like you tend the apple of your eye. Reading, thinking, speaking from the heart, feeling gratitude… All of that is fertilizer. If you stop doing it, the weeds of forgetfulness and sadness can grow.

The boy nodded thoughtfully.

Days later, while the old man rested under a tree, the boy sat beside him and began to tell him a made-up story. It was absurd and funny. The old man laughed, and that laughter rejuvenated him for a moment.

You see? the boy said proudly. I'm tending your garden.

And yours too, little one, the old man whispered.

And so, although the old man's body continued to weaken, something in his gaze grew stronger: he knew he had planted in the boy not only wisdom, but also compassion. He stood up for a moment, gazing towards the horizon, and said:

Life is like this path: the further you go, the closer you are to sunset. I don't say this with sadness, but with gratitude. Because every step leaves its mark, and when your body can no longer go on, it will be those footprints that guide your steps.

The boy lowered his gaze, trying to hide the lump in his throat.

Why are you telling me this, Grandfather?

Because time is a silent teacher, the old man replied.  And you must be prepared for when I can no longer teach you with words. There are things you will have to learn on your own, with bare feet on the stones of the path.

A dry cough interrupted his words. The old man covered his mouth with his hand, and as he did so, his eyes involuntarily moistened. The boy quickly took hold of his arm.

Rest, Grandfather, rest a little.

The old man smiled, grateful.

I will rest, son.  But promise me something: don't stop when the path grows dark. Remember that darkness exists only so we can learn to ignite our own light.

They returned and sat in the shade of a tree. The old man closed his eyes for a moment, breathing with difficulty.

The body fades, he murmured, but the soul never tires. Sometimes I feel my soul walks faster than my feet.

The boy looked at him fearfully, as if he sensed that this conversation concealed a farewell disguised as advice.

Are you going to die, Grandfather? he asked innocently.

The old man opened his eyes with infinite tenderness.

We all die, little one… but not all of us learn to live before we do. I am only preparing for the next stretch of the path. You will continue on, and when you grow weary, remember that in some corner of the wind my voice will whisper the way to you.

Silence enveloped them. Only the song of a distant bird and the whisper of the air rustling through the branches could be heard.

The body has limits, the old man continued, but the soul… the soul is infinite. That is why, even if one day my body no longer walks beside you, my spirit will continue to accompany you.

The boy took his hand, squeezing it tightly.

I don't want to go on without you, he whispered.

The old man stroked his head and replied:

It's not about going on without me... It's about continuing with me, but within you.

They remained silent for a while. The old man looked at the fire they had lit the night before, now almost extinguished, and added:

Fire also coughs before it goes out. It flickers, it sparks... but before dying, it leaves its last glow. That is what I am now, my son: a final spark. But I want my light to serve as a flame for you to ignite yours.

He looked up at the sky and, in a weaker but firm voice, said:

Sometimes I wonder if the road ends, or if it merely changes shape. Perhaps, when my time comes to leave, I will simply become part of the wind that blows through the trees, that brushes against your hair, or the echo that guides your steps.

The boy hugged him without a word.

The old man returned the gesture, knowing there was no solace for an early farewell, but there was the hope of an invisible continuity.

As they resumed walking, the old man walked slower than ever, but his gaze shone with a profound peace.

Someday, he said, you will understand that true love is not measured in time shared, but in footprints that endure.

The boy listened in silence, and without realizing it, began to memorize every word, every gesture, every step… because something inside him told him that, when the old man's body could no longer go on, the boy's soul would have to continue walking for both of them.

# CHAPTER XXII

# THE BUTTERFLY

In the stillness of early evening and in the echo of their intimacy, they decided to rest. The air had a sweet fragrance, a mixture of damp earth and wildflowers. Beside the warmth of a fire they had painstakingly managed to light, their sweaty bodies and parched throats yearned for a sip of tranquility.

The old man was tireless, and the boy indomitable. They were two beings, both concave and convex, as if they were the ideal complement to each other. The strength and vigor of the youngster, combined with the cunning and experience of the seasoned man, made them almost the perfect duo.

As the sun nearly disappeared completely, silence became their most faithful companion until, suddenly, a butterfly of indescribable beauty and color appeared before them.

Look, Grandfather, said the boy, his eyes shining, a butterfly is showing us the way! The old man looked up and followed it intently.

Not every flying sign has a direction, he

replied in a measured voice. But sometimes, the most fragile things teach us the most.

The butterfly fluttered above the path and, as if understanding its importance, flew a few meters ahead and landed on a rock. When the boy took a step toward it, it rose again, moving a little further. It was as if indicating that they should follow it.

Why does it fly like that, Grandfather? The boy asked.

Because life, the old man replied, isn't lived in a straight line. Sometimes you have to stop, other times move forward, and other times fly without any apparent direction. But the important thing is to never stop moving.

Its presence was as unexpected as it was sublime. It landed in front of them like a kind of guide. It flew with a rhythmic cadence, in time with their steps. Its flight seemed guided, as if inviting them to follow. Intrigued, they decided to accompany it.

The path grew narrower and the sunlight fainter. The butterfly, however, remained, hovering through the mist. The old man paused for a moment, gazed at the horizon, and said softly:

When a butterfly appears on the path, it's a sign of transformation. Something is about to change.

The boy looked at him, curious.

Change for better or for worse? The old man smiled tenderly.

It depends on what we carry within us. The butterfly doesn't change the path; it changes the traveler.

The butterfly moved a few meters and then stopped, as if making sure they didn't lose sight of it. Each time they paused, it stopped too, waiting patiently. It was as if it understood the travelers' weariness and respected the rhythm of their souls.

They both looked up at the same time, and for the first time, in unison, they saw the same thing on the path.

To the left, there was a kind of indecipherable, blackish image, like a long, dark stain in the air that obscured everything beyond, moving with the old man's footsteps. That shadow stretched out with the weight of his years and the last days of his life, representing the nearness of the end of his journey.

In contrast, to the right, where the boy walked, the same mark appeared, but whitish and of the opposite nature: soft, luminous, like a laugh spread across the earth. It was the promise of a whole life ahead. A blank canvas ready to be painted by the most refined artist. Two destinies, two different times walking side by side.

At the very center of both signs, and right in the heart of the path, a gray stripe was drawn. It divided and at the same time united both shadows. It was the perfect balance between the fading experience and the blossoming innocence, between what is saying goodbye and what is beginning. The old man and the child understood that they were that point of union: the link between yesterday and tomorrow, between dusk and dawn.

The butterfly fluttered above them, its invisible flight tracing the phrase that ancient philosophers had so wisely repeated:

"Carpe Diem."

It reminded them that destiny isn't chosen by running or fleeing, but by walking with balance, one day at a time, savoring each step along the way.

These two shadows represented more than their mere projection on the ground; they were the breath of life within each of them. The gray passageway was the balance of their existences, the midpoint where the old man's reason met the child's innocence, and where the spirit found meaning between them.

In that instant, Plato's allegory of the cave resonated within their consciousness. They both understood that the visible doesn't always reveal the truth, and that the invisible, on the other hand, can be the purest light that guides the soul.

As they continued onward, the butterfly, light as a sigh, paused one last time on a stone at the edge of the path. Its wings shimmered in the last rays of the sun. It rose gently over a hill and then, in a slow, ascending flight, disappeared among the orange and purple-tinged clouds.

The old man stopped and closed his eyes. The boy, amazed, asked: Why did it leave, Grandfather?

The old man looked at him tenderly and replied:

Because it had already fulfilled its purpose. Signs don't stay, son; they only appear to show us the way.

The boy lowered his gaze, and in his silence hid a mixture of sadness and understanding. The old man continued: Sometimes, life sends us a butterfly when we need it most, not to change our destiny, but to remind us that there is beauty even in endings and hope in beginnings.

They both fell silent. The wind blew softly through the trees, caressing the dying fire. The old man placed his hand on the boy's shoulder and added: Each of us has our own butterfly. It could be a memory, a person, a moment, an idea, or a dream… something that propels us forward when we feel we can go no further.

And so, beneath the sky where the moon was their witness and the firmament their refuge, the two continued walking.

The old man's shadow blended into the twilight of the night, while the child's light mingled with the first glimmers of dawn.

The path, silent and eternal, held within itself that sacred instant when life, death, and hope met in a single butterfly's flight.

On the horizon, the butterfly, now invisible to their eyes, continued to flutter above them in the realm of eternity.

Because a butterfly's flight doesn't end when it is no longer seen… it only begins to be felt in the heart of the one who follows its path.

# CHAPTER XXIII
# THE REVELATION

The sun slowly retreated, as if reluctant to leave the old man and the boy alone. Shadows lengthened along the path, and the birdsong gave way to the soft chirping of crickets.

It was the first time, since they had begun their journey, that true darkness had enveloped them.

Day had been their ally; night, until then, an unconfronted mystery.

The old man, his gaze fixed on the fading horizon, spoke in a measured voice:

The path is not only traveled in the light. One must also learn to walk in the shadows… because life is not always clearly visible.

They lit a bonfire with dry branches and patience. The fire crackled timidly at first, as if it too feared the night.

The boy, his innocence shining in his eyes, asked:

And what if the darkness enters us? The old man smiled. Then we light another fire, but within the soul.

That night, they didn't go any further. They stayed near the fire, listening to the whisper of the wind that blew through the trees like an old singer, and still talking, among other things, about that unforgettable butterfly.

The old man knew that the body doesn't always endure what the spirit desires. His hands trembled slightly, and his breathing became deeper, more measured.

The boy, without knowing it, began to watch over the old man's sleep. He covered his shoulders with the blanket they shared and watched as the fire illuminated his body, weathered by the years, and his face, tanned and etched by life.

Why does the sky look so big when it gets dark? The boy asked.

Because at night, the old man replied, one remembers how small one is, and how great one can become.

Little by little, the old man closed his eyes.

The boy imitated him.

They both let themselves be lulled by the silence, by that kind of peace that only true weariness grants.

The night embraced them without fear. The moon covered them like a mother who never sleeps, like a hen gathers her chicks under her wings, and the fire, though waning, held out long enough to remind them that even the weakest flame can conquer the darkness.

Before falling asleep, the old man murmured softly, almost to himself:

Don't fear the night, child… it too is part of the journey.

And in that instant, the child understood that darkness was not the absence of light, but the space where the soul learned to see itself.

When they awoke, the fire was only a trace of warm ash.

The fresh air of dawn brought with it the murmur of a nearby river.

The old man rose slowly, leaning on his staff, while the child stretched his arms with the energy of someone who senses something is about to happen.

They walked without speaking.

Only the murmur of the water could be heard, like a voice calling them from within. Night had passed, but its lesson remained with them: without darkness there is no light, without silence there is no revelation; and when the night is darkest, it is because dawn is closest.

Dawn had surprised them by walking along the bank of a crystal-clear river. The mist danced on the water, and the birdsong mingled with the serene murmur of the current.

The dawn unfolded over the horizon, painting the sky with shades of copper and hope. The old man and the boy walked in silence, following the river's course that danced among the trees like a luminous vein. The air smelled of damp earth and new beginnings. It was a different day, though neither of them said so.

The path is quieter today, the boy whispered.

Sometimes silence brings answers, the old

man replied softly, as if afraid of awakening something slumbering in the air. The river led them to a bend where the stones were fortunate enough to form a natural altar.

The butterfly returned, flying ahead of them again, like a thread of light weaving their story together. The old man watched as his black shadow grew heavier, while the boy's white shadow shone more brightly. They both knew, without saying a word, that the end was near.

The old man stopped, and for the first time in a long time, a tremor was felt in his hands, not from fear, but from a truth about to be revealed.

Reaching the water's edge, the old man bent down to drink.

Meanwhile, the boy threw a flat stone into the water with all his might, trying to make it bounce several times before sinking. The rock touched the water five times, creating an incredible echo. Five echoes... like the five stages of the soul they had traversed together.

The water was clear, almost transparent, reflecting the sky with a perfection that was almost painful.

Rest a little, boy, the old man said in a calm voice. The body also needs to learn to listen to silence.

The boy obeyed, sat down on a rock, and watched the water flow calmly. There was something hypnotic about its constant movement. He bent down to drink, and at that moment, something startled him: the reflection in the water didn't show his own face.

What he saw was the image of the old man.

What... what is this? he stammered, backing away in fear.

The old man smiled tenderly, without surprise.

What you see isn't always what it seems. Sometimes the path shows us what we don't yet understand.

The boy looked again, and this time, the reflection moved with the ebb and flow of the water: his own face blended with the old man's, merging little by little, as if they were a single figure breathing between the past and the future.

He took a step back, confused, while his heart

pounded like a drum in his chest, and echoed in the old man's ears.

It can't be, he whispered. The old man gazed at him, knowing this moment had to come.

Everything on the path has its reflection, boy. What you see is not a mistake… it is the truth that water cannot lie.

The boy looked again, this time more calmly.

The reflection swayed with the river's waves: one moment it was his face, the next the old man's, as if they shared a single breath.

The old man observed him in silence. Then, with a look full of tenderness and truth, he said:

Do not fear, son of destiny. The water only shows what you already are, even if you do not yet understand it.

The boy looked at him, uncomprehending.

The old man continued, watching the river's steady flow:

You have seen many things since we began

our journey. You remember the woman on the path, the one who sought love in a face that did not see her… She taught you that one cannot continue moving forward with a chained heart. Do you remember the map, the one that never marked a destination, only a direction… because the purpose isn't at the end, but in every step?

And the magic hole, where what was lost didn't disappear, but changed shape?

The truth that is sold, the market where conscience had a price, the castles in the air you built without foundations… All of that was you, searching for yourself in every reflection.

The boy listened, unable to tear his gaze away from the water. His reflection began to blend with the old man's, moving with the waves as if they were one, trapped between time and eternity.

And the unsung heroes? the boy asked, his voice trembling.

The old man smiled.

They were the hands that held you without you seeing them. The Simon of Cyrene who helped you carry the weight when you could go no further.

They are all part of the same spirit that guides us, even though their names are lost in the wind.

The wind blew, as if answering his words, and the forest trembled. The old man looked up and continued in a deeper tone: The valley of dry bones showed you that even the dead can live again if faith is infused into them.

The tower that watches over the footsteps taught you that conscience is always watching, even when you think you are alone.

And the parallel between the path and life… revealed to you that what you tread on outside is only a reflection of what you build within.

The boy stared at him, speechless. The old man waded a little deeper into the river, and for a moment, his figure seemed to dissolve into the reflection.

I have walked through all those places, he said, but I didn't walk them with you for the first time. I had already experienced them before. And each time I experienced them, I learned the same thing again: that the soul does not die, it only repeats itself until it remembers who it is.

The boy shuddered.

So… you knew all this would happen? The old man nodded slowly.

Because I've already lived it. Because you and I are the same traveler at different dawns of time. You are my beginning, and I am your end. The path brought us together so that the circle could close.

The boy's eyes widened in confusion as he tried to make sense of it.

But… if we are the same, how can we walk together?

The path has its mysteries, the old man replied. Sometimes life allows us to see ourselves reflected in our own stages so that we understand who we truly are. Time not only moves forward, it also folds back on itself, like a river returning to its source.

The old man continued:

Every step you take, I have already taken. Every mistake you make, I have made. But every truth you discover will also be new to me. Because the soul does not age; it only transforms.

The boy tried to speak, but the words wouldn't come. The revelation overwhelmed him. Everything they had experienced the mountains, the butterfly, the nights of reflection by the fire took on a new meaning.

Time is not always a straight line, the old man continued. Sometimes it bends back on itself so that the soul can come face to face with its truth. I, too, was a child searching for answers. I walked, I stumbled, and I learned… until one day I met you.

There was a long silence. Only the murmur of the river filled the air, as if the water, too, understood the mystery.

The boy looked at his reflection again: he saw neither the old man nor himself, but a single figure, serene and luminous.

The old man spoke to him in a low but firm voice:

When the time comes, the butterfly will return. She knows the path that leads to the bridge. There, footsteps dissolve, and only the soul continues. But do not fear… the time is not yet. There is still light to walk upon and paths to understand. A time will come when the master must stay behind so that the disciple may walk alone, he said at last. But that day has not yet arrived. I still have things to teach you, and you still have things to discover.

The boy wanted to ask more, but he couldn't.

The river, the wind, and the silence enveloped everything.

They both remained still, contemplating the flow of the water, knowing that something had changed forever. The old man stood up, gazed at the horizon, and said:

Let's go on, son of the road. Truth doesn't end at the riverbank… it extends beyond the bridge.

And they began to walk.

The boy was beside him, and the butterfly the one that seemed forgotten reappeared, flying ahead of them, guiding them toward the radiance that awaited them further on.

They didn't speak because there was no need.

The river continued its course, reflecting two shadows that time, little by little, would unite into one. And as the sun rose over the horizon, they both resumed their journey.

It wasn't the end of the road, but the beginning of a new awareness. The road doesn't end at the last hill or at the horizon that disappears from sight. The road continues within each being, in every step we take, in every doubt, and in every faith that sustains us.

The child and the old man were not two different travelers, but rather a reflection of what we all carry within: the innocence that drives us to dream and the experience that invites us to remember.

And amidst these two voices, the true traveler learns that to live is to unite what seems opposed, to reconcile what we thought was divided, to mend what seems broken, and to move forward with a whole heart. No goal is worthwhile if the soul is left behind. No abyss is too deep, no tunnel too dark, when one walks with purpose.

Thus, the lesson of the journey is simple and eternal: we are many in one, but we can walk as one. And as long as the steps continue, the horizon will always offer new paths, new lights, new lessons. Because the journey, in truth, never ends.

The journey…is you.

# CHAPTER XXIV

# THE BRIDGE

Dawn greeted them with a peculiar silence, and the path opened onto a different horizon, brighter, quieter, as if the world were holding its breath.

The boy and the old man walked beneath a light mist that drifted across the grass, marking their footsteps with golden light. They advanced among gentle hills covered in flowers that seemed to breathe everything.

They had traveled so far... and yet, that morning felt like the beginning of something greater.

The air smelled of eternity. There was neither sun nor shadow, only a clarity that came from nowhere, but illuminated everything.

They walked for a long time without speaking, feeling each step grow lighter, as if the weight of years and doubts were left behind with the dust of the path.

The butterfly flew ahead of them, moving

among the petals like a flicker of living memory, guiding them toward a radiance that grew with each step.

The landscape slowly changed. And the path began to open into a valley that seemed suspended between heaven and earth.

The flowers grew taller, almost transparent, as if light were emanating from within them, as if they were holding hands. And then, before them, rose an immense garden, a valley of impossible colors where silence had a voice and the air seemed made of ancient sighs.

In the center of the garden, an arc of light rose. It was similar to the one they had crossed at the beginning of their journey, but now it radiated a deeper beauty, as if all they had experienced had prepared them to understand its true meaning.

The old man stopped. His gaze, serene and weary, was filled with a peace the boy had never seen. And his eyes, exhausted yet luminous, recognized the end of their journey.

The garden led them to a great bridge shrouded in mist, suspended over the unknown. The old man stopped, looking at it with a certain doubt, but also with serenity. For a moment, he thought he wasn't sure where it would lead him, but he understood that when you live a clean life, without harming others, with a peaceful soul and a tranquil relationship with the world, eternal rest becomes as clear as water. He smiled, aware that one dies as one lives, and that the bridge only reflects what has been sown in the heart.

We have reached the threshold, boy, he said softly. The path doesn't end... it only changes shape.

The boy gazed at the rainbow of light, marveling.

What's on the other side? he asked.

The old man smiled tenderly.

Some call it rest, others call it return, and others call it eternity. But in truth, it is the beginning of all that never ends.

In front of the arch, the floor was made of glass, and beneath it were reflected infinite images: faces, places, moments of the journey, and even voices.

There was the woman from the road, with her

hopeful gaze; Simon of Cyrene, bearing his invisible burden; the unsung heroes, smiling among the crowd; the butterfly, dancing on the wind; and the echoes of memory, whispering fragments of what they had lived.

Every story they had crossed, every soul, every lesson… awaited them on the other side. The boy took a step forward, but the old man stopped him.

Not yet, child of destiny.

Each one crosses the bridge when the key is complete.

The key? The boy asked.

Yes, the old man replied. It is not made of metal, but of deeds. The key is forged from who we are: our actions, our deeds, our faith, our loves, our falls, our wounds… and the way we choose to heal. All of that is part of the key that opens this door.

Only those who have loved without measure and learned without fear can open the arch of eternity.

The boy remained silent.

He looked at his hands, then at the old man's, and understood that both were the same story written in different eras.

And what if someone arrives without a key? the boy asked, his voice trembling. The old man looked at him tenderly and spoke slowly:

Then the garden invites them to return.

Not as punishment, but as a second chance.

No one is rejected here. It's just that some must continue learning to love before crossing over.

So... you already have your key, Grandfather? The old man smiled, without answering.

A tear, thin and transparent, slid down his cheek.

Perhaps, he said, but the important thing isn't crossing first... but having walked together to get here.

And he added in a trembling voice:

I hope, my son, that when you reach the other side of the bridge, you will have lived enough. I hope that love will sustain you completely. And when they let you in, may you do so lightly, without guilt, without fear, without baggage. May they let you in with all that you were when you arrive. With your doubts, your mistakes, your dreams, and your faith. Because all of that is also love, and love opens all doors.

The boy felt his heart clench.

The old man embraced him with a tenderness that seemed infinite.

Look, son, he whispered. The butterfly will show you the way when your time comes. I only went as far as I was meant to.

The important thing isn't arriving... It's conquering the pathway.

Then the wind blew from the garden, and for a moment, everything was filled with light.

The boy saw figures among the flowers: they were those who had left, those who had once loved and been loved.

Their faces showed not sadness, but welcome. The old man gazed at them with gratitude. They crossed over before, he said. They're waiting for us on the other side. Each will arrive when their key allows it.

The butterfly landed on the boy's shoulder and then flew toward the arc of light. The old man watched it go and sighed.

You see, even wings have their time. Silence enveloped them.

The old man walked toward the light. He took one step, then another. Each step became lighter, more transparent, more eternal.

The light from the arc touched him, and for an instant, his body became transparent, as if made of breeze and memories.

The boy wanted to stop him, but something inside told him not to.

The old man looked at him one last time, and in a voice that seemed to come from the wind, said:

We will meet again. Every true path leads to reunion.

The boy watched him until his figure merged with the light.

Then he understood: the bridge wasn't outside, but inside the heart. At that same instant, the boy closed his eyes.

When he opened them, the old man was gone.

Only his shadow remained, blending with the garden's light… and the walking stick, leaning gently against a rock, as if waiting for its owner.

The boy picked it up, held it reverently, and gazed toward the archway.

The butterfly was still fluttering there, waiting for him, but he knew his time had not yet come.

He sat among the flowers, gazing at the horizon. And then he understood that the path is not conquered with the feet… but with the soul. That every step, every fall, every love, and every loss had been part of the same learning process. That it wasn't about arriving first, but about arriving fully awake.

And that eternity doesn't begin after death, but when the heart learns to live without fear.

Thus ended his journey, not with a goodbye, but with a profound understanding: that the path doesn't end, it only changes shape. And that the conquest lies not in reaching the goal, but in having been transformed by it.

# ABOUT THE AUTHOR

José Galván is a thoughtful voice shaped by both intellectual discipline and deep personal reflection. With a Bachelor of Science in Accounting (1996) from the Technological University of Santiago (UTESA) and an Associate of Science in Computer Science (1992) from the Pedro Henríquez Ureña University (UNPHU), his academic journey reflects a balance between logic and introspection.

Beyond his professional formation, José Galván is a keen observer of life's inner pathways, the silent struggles, the lessons hidden in time, and the wisdom that emerges from both beginnings and endings. *Conquering the Pathway* is not merely a literary work, but a reflection of his philosophical outlook: that life is a journey shaped not only by external steps, but by the evolution of the soul.

Through his writing, he seeks not to instruct, but to accompany, to offer readers a mirror in which they may recognize their own experiences, questions, and hopes. His work resonates with those who understand that the greatest journeys are not measured in distance, but in awareness, growth, and the courage to continue forward.